Exploring Washington on Foot

*Twelve Hikes Between
Metro Stops*

By Bob Bruton

Rockrose Publications

Washington, D.C.

Copyright © 1995 by Robert H. Bruton

Requests for permission to reproduce selections from this book should be addressed to Bob Bruton, 2556 Virginia Ave., N.W., Suite 198, Washington, DC 20037

IBSN 0-9647813-0-1

Published by

Rockrose Publications
Washington, D.C.

What This Book Is About

A few years back my wife and I quit our jobs, dusted off our hiking boots and backpacking gear, and set out to explore the wilds of North America. When we returned to Washington a year later, very fit from trekking up and down hills and mountains, we tried to maintain the exercise and pleasure of hiking. But the mountains are far away, and it's a bother to get things arranged and pack up the car, and ....

And then we discovered the city.

It started mostly as a matter of practicality. Not only is Washington close at hand, but it also provides a perfect solution to a basic problem in hiking. Unless you have an extra car or are willing to gamble on the possibility of catching a ride with a stranger, hiking always means spending half your time and energy getting back to where you started, often retracing your steps.

Washington's Metro system solves this problem beautifully: You can simply hike from one Metro station to another and rely on the subway to get you quickly and easily back to your starting point. But while that solves an important practical problem, it raises a bigger question: What pleasure is to be had in hiking around a busy, noisy city?

Well, Washington is not, of course, all busy and noisy. Indeed it is a wonderland of quiet streets, lovely parks, elegant old buildings, shaded neighborhoods, plus a little of the exciting and the unusual. The objective, therefore, is to find hiking routes between Metro stations that offer the hiker the best of the city. That's what this book is all about.

While putting together the hikes in this book, we came to look upon the city as a part of nature; not wilderness, certainly, but as much a natural creation as a wood or a stream. We still leave the city now and again to hike the mountains, but we also love to hike the city. And we have found that, like the particular pleasure of hiking through blooming mountain laurel in a grove of hemlock, there is a particular pleasure in hiking past finely nurtured gardens bordering a stand of row houses that have gathered a patina of age and history and care.

And the exercise is every bit as good in the city as it is in the mountains.

Bob Bruton

Comments, Please

Any comments readers may have on this book would be greatly appreciated. I am particularly interested in updates to route directions and suggestions for new hikes to be included in later editions. Please send your comments to Bob Bruton, 2556 Virginia Ave., N.W., Suite 198, Washington, DC 20037.

Acknowledgments

This book would not have been possible without the careful, thoughtful, and imaginative editing of Paul Mathless. Reading his detailed markup of the manuscript was one long lesson in good writing. To have had such professional help was a godsend. Any mistakes or absence of clarity that remain in the text after Paul's edit are entirely my own fault.

Other invaluable help was the final proofreading provided by Mollie Weinert and the long-term help and encouragement given by my wife Rina.

Providing good company on the hikes and helping to check out routes and directions were: Paul, Mollie, Rina, my good friends Mike Nagy and Tom Roland, my daughter Deirdre Messenger, and my sister Sally Harris.

Finally, Jim Lawson, who paved the way by creating several books of his own, helped me with the many practical details of publishing.

Neither the author nor the publisher can be held responsible for the experiences of the reader while taking the hikes described in this book.

Table of Contents

INTRODUCTION

THE HIKES

This book describes twelve hikes -- ranging in length from 5.6 to 10.4 miles -- you can take through the city and suburbs of Washington, D.C. Each hike begins at one Metro station and ends at another. The hikes normally take at least a morning or an afternoon to complete and some may take the better part of a day. All are long enough to provide useful exercise, but they are well within the capabilities of people in reasonably good health.

The hikes take you to a lot of interesting, unusual, and beautiful places: past monuments, statues, embassies, and historic sites both famous and barely known; on dirt trails through wooded parkland; down busy avenues of commerce, entertainment, and nightlife; along quiet, tree-lined streets of historic neighborhoods; through university campuses, cemeteries, and military posts; past much grand and some fanciful architecture.

They are also laid out to provide you with some practical necessities. Each route includes rest stops and, usually, some convenient public rest rooms along the way. I've also listed places to eat or get a drink, particularly at or near the end of the hike where you can celebrate your accomplishment. These are mostly the kind of places where a hiker -- tired and maybe a little dusty and sweaty -- will feel welcome.

USING THIS GUIDEBOOK

Each hike makes up a separate chapter. The first part of each chapter gives information to help you select and plan a hike -- basic data such as starting and ending points, length, and time to complete the hike; highlights of what you will encounter along the route; an overall route map; identification of rest stops, rest rooms, and places to eat; and any special cautions you should note. The second part presents information to be read en route -- route directions (with detailed map inserts) along with descriptions of many of the places of interest you will encounter.

GENERAL PREPARATIONS AND PRECAUTIONS

Following the Hiking Routes

Following directions through city streets is probably more challenging than following trails in the wilds, because the city offers so many possible routes. And I caution that it may be especially easy to get lost taking the hikes in this guidebook, since the routes are designed to be circuitous. Follow the directions carefully. If you get lost, see the section below: "What To Do If You Get Lost." Even though this book includes many detailed maps of each route, you should also carry a street map of the city in case you wander off the route. If you are not familiar with the city, make sure you read the section below, "Washington's Street Pattern."

A special problem in any city guidebook is that directions usually must be keyed to manmade signs and landmarks that are anything but permanent. Therefore, try to avoid relying on any single sign or landmark.

Also, routes may be temporarily blocked or altered due to construction activity. The detours you will need to take in these cases are usually simple and obvious. Occasionally, however, -- for example, when a bridge is closed -- you may be forced into a long and not so obvious detour, or you may even be forced to abandon the hike until a more opportune time. Having a good street map in these situations is particularly useful.

Traffic Safety

In following the routes presented in this guidebook you will need to cross many roads and highways. The vehicular traffic patterns and controls and the pedestrian protections at many of these crossings are complex and confusing and may change from time to time. I specifically caution you not to assume that the directions given in this guidebook always represent a safe way to enter or cross a roadway. As you proceed along any route following the directions, particularly before you enter or cross roadways, make your own on-the-spot safety assessment and change the route if necessary.

In a number of places in this guidebook, I have inserted cautionary notes. These notes describe some, but not necessarily all, situations where you should exercise special care. The absence of a cautionary note does not mean that you should proceed without caution. As you will, I hope, be exploring terra incognita, you should never turn off your alertness or good sense.

Street Crime

As most experienced city dwellers know, the chance of encountering street crime very much depends on where you are and the time of day. While I certainly cannot guarantee your safety, I can say, as a long time resident here, that the hikes in this book all pass through parts of the city where I feel comfortable walking during daylight. But places that are safe during the day may not be so at night. It is a good idea, therefore, to make sure you begin each hike in time to finish before dark. The next section gives some tips on how to plan for this.

Estimating Distance and Duration

The total distance of each hike is shown at the beginning of the hike description. Also, each direction en route is tagged with the distance remaining to the end of the hike. Distances are given to the nearest tenth of a mile. A distance followed by a minus sign means that the associated direction is farther on, but by less than a tenth of a mile, than the previous direction.

The length of time it takes to complete a hike can only be roughly estimated, since it can vary widely depending on how fast you walk and how many times, and for how long, you stop. To help you estimate, I give an example duration with each hike description, along with the walking speed and number and duration of stops upon which it is based. If you are a determined hiker who walks at a faster pace and makes fewer or shorter stops, you will complete the hike in a much shorter time. A leisurely pace and more and longer stops will considerably lengthen the time. Unless you are taking the hike primarily for the exercise and have little or no interest in the places along the route, you should probably assume that the hike will take you at least as long as the example duration given with the hike description.

The Weather

With the proper clothing, hiking is practical any time of the year. Most people, however, will want to hike in warm weather. In Washington that usually means from early April, when the cherry trees are blooming, to late October, when the fall colors are fading. By far the best weather in Washington is in the spring and fall. In fact, Washington can produce some spectacularly beautiful days during these seasons. But many people end up hiking in summer.

In the summer months, cities are hot places to hike in, and Washington is a notoriously hot city. While I looked for shade in laying out the hikes, some routes offer little shade and every route has stretches in the sun. This being the case, there are precautions you can take when hiking in hot weather.

First, on days when hot weather is predicted, avoid the hikes that have a lot of heat exposure. These are identified under each hike in the section entitled "Some Cautions." Second, carry water and rest frequently. I list places to rest in the description of each hike. Third, take advantage of the available air conditioning when you feel you need to escape the heat. Many of the hikes pass public buildings that are air-conditioned. All the hikes pass air-conditioned restaurants where you can stop to cool off and get a bottled water or a soft drink.

Washington is also subject to sudden and sometimes violent thunderstorms, particularly in hot weather. Some of the hikes pass through areas where shelter is readily available, but some do not, and the prudent hiker will, therefore, take some rain gear. Storms usually come in late afternoon and approach from the north and west. When the sky darkens in those directions, look for shelter.

If you hike in cold weather, most of the above cautions do not apply. But a different problem accompanies winter hiking. Public rest rooms and drinking fountains that are not protected from the cold are closed.

Clothing and Footwear

During the hot season the basic rule is to dress for the heat and be prepared for the rain. This usually means wearing loose-fitting clothes and a broad-brimmed hat and carrying a lightweight rain parka.

Footwear is a special concern due to the length of the hikes and the hard walking surfaces. Except in a few places on a few hikes, traction is not important. What is important is cushioning the hot, tired soles of your feet. High quality sneakers or walking shoes provide good protection. But the best choice of all might be the new, high-quality (and expensive) soft-rubber-soled sandals designed specifically for outdoor use. Whatever you wear on your feet, however, make sure a long hike is not the first time you have worn them.

Good socks are almost as important as good shoes. Strange as it may seem, heavy wool socks can be better than light cotton socks because of wool's greater cushioning and its ability to draw perspiration away from the feet. Some synthetic materials have the same properties. And if you have especially tender feet or if you just want to treat your feet to special comfort, get yourself a pair of thin silk sock liners, sold at most outdoors equipment stores, to wear under your other socks.

Although the right footwear will probably protect your feet adequately, it is a good idea to take along something to protect blisters if you get them.

WHAT TO DO IF YOU GET LOST

The first thing to do if you get lost is to identify in the hike description the last direction you are <u>sure</u> you passed correctly. Most directions are identified with a location and you will have to return to the location of this last identified direction. Perhaps a passerby can tell you how to get there. If not, try to figure out where you are based on street signs. If you know where you are, you can often get to where you want to be by using your knowledge of the street pattern. See the section on Washington's street pattern below.

The next best thing to getting directions from a helpful passerby is to have a good street map. The one-page maps at the beginning of each chapter may also help.

If you get lost within the Metro system, ask for help from an attendant on duty. If you are having trouble finding the right exit from a station, make sure you ask for help before you pass through the fare card gates.

WASHINGTON'S STREET PATTERN

The city of Washington is divided into four quadrants of radically unequal size: Northwest, Northeast, Southwest, and Southeast. The hikes are mostly in Northwest, the largest quadrant, but some pass through Southwest and Southeast. The four quadrants meet at the Capitol. Within the quadrants, most streets are laid out in a rectangular grid pattern. The north-and-south streets are numbered, with the numbers increasing as you move east or west away from the Capitol. Lettered streets run east-and-west and are ordered alphabetically. As you move north or south away from the Capitol, you run first through the alphabet of single letter streets, then through an alphabet of two-syllable names, then three-syllable names, and, finally, in the far reaches of Northwest, an alphabet of tree or flower names.

This is about as much as can be said for the logic of Washington's street system. Now for the illogic. There are many avenues, named mostly for states, that cross the rectangular pattern of streets at many odd angles. There is no pattern whatever to these avenues. The system of rectangular streets and angling avenues is part of the original grand plan for the city laid down by Pierre L'Enfant. Unfortunately, as the city expanded, the developers of new neighborhoods and subdivisions did not always follow L'Enfant's grand plan. A few neighborhoods have their own, unique street pattern. In other cases, streets follow the L'Enfant plan but with deviations that seem designed to confuse outsiders. Finally, the street systems of the adjoining Virginia and Maryland suburbs bear little or no relationship to the L'Enfant plan.

HOW TO USE METRO

If you are a newcomer to Washington, the following instructions on how to use the Metro system may be helpful.

To find a Metro station look for the brown-painted, square-sided steel columns marked with a large white letter "M" that are normally located near each entrance. Unfortunately, these entrance markers are often not very obvious amid the street clutter and you may be quite close to a station before you see one.

Once in a station, find one of the many Metro system maps posted throughout the system. On this map, find the station you are currently in and the station you want to go to. Then identify the lines and transfer points connecting those stations. Metro lines are identified by color (red, blue, orange, green, and yellow). Direction on a line is identified by the name of the final station. For example, to ride from the Silver Spring station to Arlington Cemetery station, you take the red line in the direction of Shady Grove and get off at Metro Center, where you transfer to the blue line in the direction of Van Dorn Street.

To pass through the fare card gates leading to the train platforms, each person must have a fare card. To buy a fare card, use one of the fare card machines that are available in each station. These machines accept nickels, dimes, quarters, and bills up to $20.00. The fares required to ride from the station you are currently in to any other station in the system are posted at the bottom of a Metro system map located near the fare card machines and on kiosks next to the fare card gates. Fares depend on distance between stations and time of day; most fares are higher during weekday rush hours. You can buy a fare card for any amount from the minimum fare (presently $1.10) to $20.00, but you should buy a card with at least the value required for the ride you are about to take.

Once each person has a fare card, you can pass through the fare card gates by inserting the fare card in the slot in the front side of a gate. The fare card gate opens, electronically marks your card, and returns it to you through a slot in its top side. If you do not have the minimum fare on your fare card, the gate will return your card without opening.

Now you must find your way to the proper train platform. Follow the directions posted in the station to the line <u>and</u> <u>direction</u> you want (e.g., red line to Shady Grove). In the larger stations serving more than one line, this may prove to be a challenging task. Follow the signs carefully. And the challenge is not over even when you reach your platform, since some platforms serve two lines. Thus, before boarding a train, make sure it is on the right line and going in the right direction. The line color and direction are usually posted on the outside of the train. Also, the motorman will call out the line and direction on the train's public address system (e.g., "This is a red line train to Shady Grove.")

Once you are on the train, each upcoming station is called out by the motorman (e.g., "The next station is Arlington

Cemetery."). There are also signs identifying each station that can be seen through the train windows.

When you alight from the train at your destination station, you usually face a choice of several station exits. The hike directions in this book direct you to one specific exit. Make sure you are headed toward the right exit before you pass through the fare card gates.

When you pass through the fare card gates on exiting the Metro system, the fare is subtracted from the amount on your fare card. If there is any amount remaining on your fare card after this subtraction, the card is returned to you. If the amount on your fare card is insufficient, the gate will not open and you will need to add the deficiency to your fare card at an "exitfare" or "addfare" machine.

If you need help, ask the attendant on duty at each bank of fare card gates.

SOME OTHER SOURCES OF INFORMATION

The following books, pamphlets, and maps provide additional information about the Washington area. Much of the information used in this book was derived from these sources.

Things to Take with You When Hiking

All About the Metro System. The Washington Metropolitan Area Transit Authority.

> A pamphlet with the latest information on fares, scheduled frequencies, hours of service and station entrance closings, and a map of the system. Available free from Metrorail Information. (202) 637-7000.

Let's Meet Near Metro, by Jim C. Lawson. Ardmore Publications, 1994.

> A pocket-size guide to restaurants within two blocks of Metro stations; makes a good gastronomic companion to this guidebook. Local bookstores.

The Walker Washington Guide, by John and Katharine Walker. EPM Publications, 1991.

> A comprehensive pocket-size tourist guide to Washington, with lots of detail about the city's major attractions. Local bookstores.

Washington, D.C. Transportation Map. Office of Policy and Planning, District of Columbia Department of Public Works.

> A detailed map of the city and its inner suburbs, covering the routes of all the hikes in this guidebook; a good map to take with you on the hikes. Available free from the D.C. Committee to Promote Washington. (202) 724-4091.

Things to Read Before or After Hiking

Footnote Washington, by Bryson B. Rash.   EPM Publications, 1983.

> A collection of mostly humorous anecdotes about some of the city's sites, written by a longtime Washington journalist. Local bookstores.

The Guide to Black Washington, by Sandra Fitzpatrick and Maria R. Goodwin. Hippocrene Books, 1990.

> A comprehensive guide to significant sites in Washington's African American history. Local bookstores.

Natural Washington, by Richard L. Berman and Deborah Gerhard. EPM Publications, Inc., 1980.

> A book describing natural areas in and around the nation's capital. Local bookstores.

On this Spot - Pinpoint the Past in Washington, D.C., by Douglas E. Evelyn and Paul Dickson. Farragut Publishing Company, 1992.

> A historical atlas of the District of Columbia. Local bookstores.

Washington on Foot, edited by John J. Protopappas and Alvin R. McNeal. Smithsonian Institution Press, 1992.

> A book presenting twenty-one short walks through Washington; especially good for its architectural descriptions. Local bookstores.

The Washington Historical Atlas, by Laura Bergheim. Woodbine House, 1992.

> A comprehensive atlas of historical sites in the District of Columbia. Local bookstores.

Washington at Home, edited by Kathryn Schneider Smith. Windsor Publications, Inc., 1988.

> A history of twenty-one Washington neighborhoods. Available at local bookstores and from the Historical Society of Washington, D.C. (202) 785-2068.

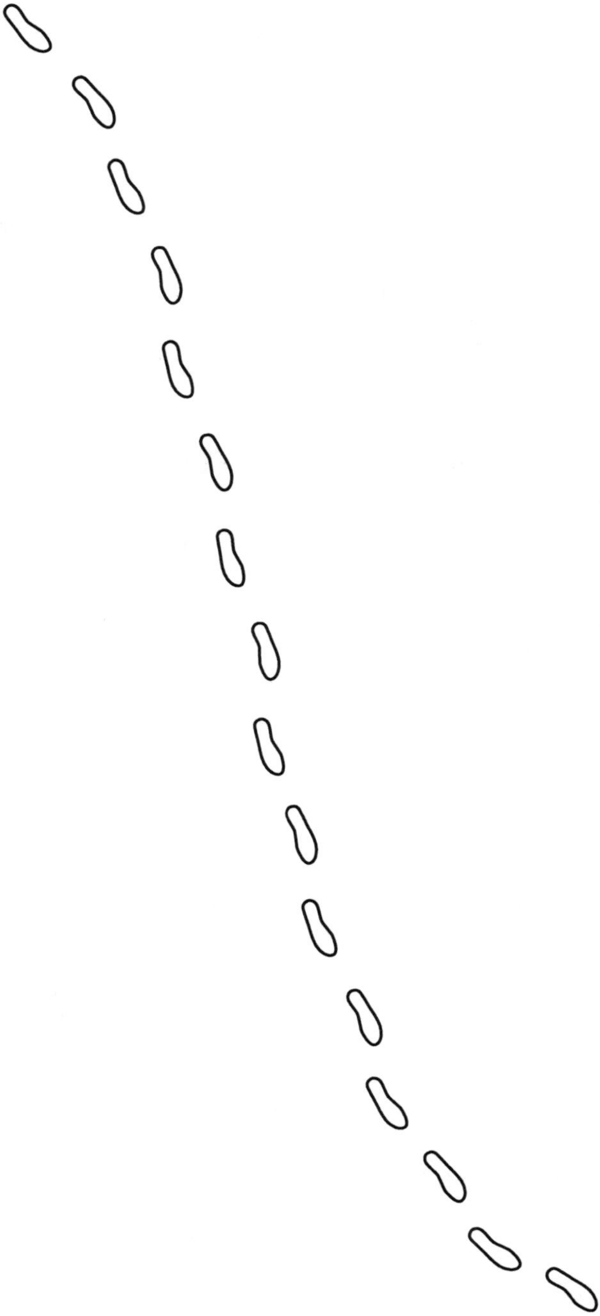

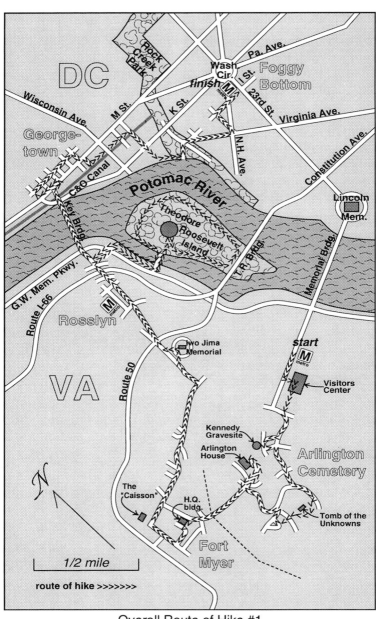

Overall Route of Hike #1
Arlington Cemetery to Foggy Bottom

HIKE #1

Graves of heros; honor guards and their horses; an island wilderness; an infamous flight of steps; historic row houses; a canal boat and mules to tow it; a riverside boardwalk; and a modern political scandal.

From: Arlington Cemetery Metro Station (Virginia)

To: Foggy Bottom Metro Station (D.C.)

Via: Arlington National Cemetery, the U.S. Army post at Fort Myer, the Rosslyn neighborhood of Arlington, Va., Theodore Roosevelt Island in the Potomac River, Francis Scott Key Bridge, Georgetown, the Chesapeake and Ohio Canal, the Washington Harbour development, the Watergate complex, and Washington's Foggy Bottom neighborhood.

Distance: 8.6 miles

Duration: 5½ hours if you walk at 2.5 miles per hour, make eight 10-minute stops, and take a 45-minute break for lunch.

Highlights

From the Arlington Cemetery Metro Station, the hike meanders along the shaded lanes of Arlington National Cemetery past the John F. Kennedy gravesite, with its eternal flame, the Tomb of the Unknowns, with its perpetual honor guard, and Robert E. Lee's Arlington House. From the cemetery you will walk through Fort Myer, home of the honor guard and the Army's last horses, and then to the U.S. Marine Corps (Iwo Jima) Memorial. After passing through the modern high-rise neighborhood of Rosslyn, home of *USA Today*, the hike takes you a short distance down the Virginia bank of the Potomac River and then across a footbridge to the wooded parkland of Theodore Roosevelt Island. On the island you will visit the lovely, secluded memorial to the conservationist president and then hike on dirt trails through hardwood forest and marshes. Returning to the Virginia bank of the river, you will cross the Key Bridge, leaving Virginia and entering the District of Columbia at Georgetown. There you will pass a historic streetcar barn and then make the long climb up the flight of stairs made infamous in the movie "The Exorcist" into the heart of a beautifully restored and very pricey residential neighborhood. Passing from the residential to the once industrial part of Georgetown, you will walk for a short way along the towpath of the historic Chesapeake and Ohio Canal. In warm weather, a mule drawn canal boat operates here. Leaving the canal, you will walk among the buildings and fountains, and down the riverbank boardwalk of the architecturally controversial Washington Harbour development. You will then leave the river behind and walk up Virginia Avenue between the Watergate complex and the Howard Johnson Motor Lodge, both made notorious during the Nixon presidency. Finally, you will pass the quaint row houses of the once disreputable but now high-rent Foggy Bottom neighborhood, before ending the hike at the Foggy Bottom Metro Station.

Things to Know Before You Start

All distances shown in parentheses below indicate miles to the end of the hike.

Intermediate Metro Stations

If you get tired, the Rosslyn Metro Station (4.7 miles) makes a handy bail-out point about half way through the hike. See Map 1-5.

Places to Stop for a Rest

By far the best place to take a break is at the memorial on Theodore Roosevelt Island (3.9 miles). This is a wonderfully shaded and quiet spot surrounded by a ring-shaped pond and provided with many benches. It is a little beyond the middle of the hike. Other convenient rest spots are: the amphitheater adjacent to the Tomb of the Unknowns (7.5 miles); Arlington House (6.9 miles); the Marine Corps memorial (5.1 miles); and Washington Harbour (0.8 miles).

Places to Stop and Eat

The premier way to eat on this hike is to picnic at the memorial on Theodore Roosevelt Island (3.9 miles). You can either bring your own food or pick up some carry-out at the excellent delicatessen in the shopping mall next to the Rosslyn Metro Station (4.7 miles). (See Map 1-5, page 24.) The mall also has a few fast food shops, but they may not be open on weekends. If you prefer to be served, the mall boasts an excellent, but possibly a bit formal, restaurant.

There is also an informal restaurant at the top of the "Exorcist" steps (1.5 miles). Within easy reach of Potomac and M Streets (1.2 miles) -- in the Georgetown Market, in the Georgetown Park shopping mall, and along M Street -- are a variety of places to eat. At the Washington Harbour (0.8 miles), on the bank of the river, is another, smaller, cluster of restaurants. Finally, two suitable, small restaurants are located in the Watergate complex (0.5 miles).

Public Rest Rooms

Relief is available at the following places along the route: the Arlington Cemetery Visitors Center (8.5 miles); Arlington House (6.9 miles); the shopping mall next to the Rosslyn Metro Station (4.7 miles); on Theodore Roosevelt Island (3.6 miles), in Georgetown Park (1.2 miles), and in the Watergate shopping mall (0.5 miles). In a pinch, portable toilets are usually stationed at the memorial on Theodore Roosevelt Island (3.9 miles).

Some Cautions

This is one of the longer hikes and it includes some climbing up and down hills. The long, steep, "Exorcist" steps are particularly challenging.

The hike on Theodore Roosevelt Island follows dirt trails that are usually muddy in places. In summer, these trails may take you past patches of poison ivy and stinging nettles.

On-Route Directions After You Start

Numbers in the left margin indicate miles to the end of the hike. Unless otherwise indicated, maps are oriented north to top of page.

8.6   Two exits lead up to street level from the Arlington Cemetery Metro Station. Take the one that is on the left after you pass through the Metro fare card gates. When you reach street level at the top of the escalator, you are facing west toward the formal marble entrance to Arlington National Cemetery, with Memorial Bridge, the Lincoln Memorial, and the Washington Monument at your back. Walk west toward the formal entrance to the Cemetery.

Arlington National Cemetery is the final resting place of more than a quarter million servicemen and women and members of their immediate families. Presidents Taft and Kennedy are buried here, along with a number of Medal of Honor winners -- the best known probably being Audie Murphy, movie star and the most decorated serviceman of World War II. The cemetery began in the early years of the Civil War with the burial of Union soldiers on the grounds of the estate vacated by Robert E. Lee and his family. The property was initially confiscated on the grounds that the Lees failed to pay taxes in person -- an obvious impossibility during the war. Many years after the war, the Supreme Court ordered that the family be compensated.

8.5   About halfway to the formal entrance, after crossing a road to your left leading to a parking area, go left (south) at the sign that says Arlington National Cemetery, through a set of iron gates, to the cemetery visitors center. There are public rest rooms and drinking fountains here. You can also pick up a map of the cemetery.

8.4   Leave the visitors center through the doors that were to your right (west) when you entered. Outside, follow the walkway that begins a few steps to your right and leads away from the visitors center.

8.3   Where the walkway ends, cross the perpendicular road and then follow the unmarked road leading diagonally to the left. This is Roosevelt Avenue.

8.1   At the first intersecting street leading to the right, turn right. This is Weeks Avenue. It leads uphill to the Kennedy grave site. (See Map 1-1.)

8.0   Where Weeks Avenue merges with an unmarked road (Sheridan Avenue) from the right, continue straight up a short ramp or flight of steps to the

Kennedy gravesite. Return to this point after visiting the gravesite. (See Map 1-1.)

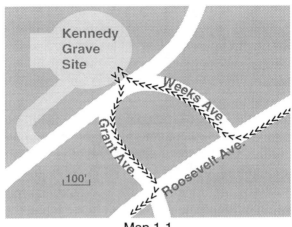

Map 1-1

The mansion on the hilltop above the Kennedy gravesite is Lee's home, Arlington House. You will visit the mansion later in this hike.

8.0   On leaving the grave site down the same steps or ramp you went up, follow the unmarked road (Grant Avenue) leading diagonally off to your right. Do not follow the road immediately to your right. (See Map 1-1.) In a short distance, you should pass the Tourmobile bus stop.

If you look to your right on Grant Avenue and around the next turn on Roosevelt Avenue, you will find the gravestones of many famous high-ranking military leaders, including Daniel "Chappie" James, Jr., of the Air Force, who was the first African American four-star general, and the polar explorer Admiral Richard E. Byrd, Jr.

7.9   At the first intersection, where Grant Avenue crosses Roosevelt Avenue, turn right onto Roosevelt. There is a small sign here pointing down Roosevelt Avenue to the Tomb of the Unknowns. (See Map 1-1.)

7.8   Where Roosevelt Avenue intersects McClellan Avenue, continue straight on Roosevelt. Again, there is a sign pointing ahead, along Roosevelt Avenue, to the Tomb of the Unknowns.

7.7   At the intersection of Wilson Avenue with Roosevelt
        Avenue, continue straight on Roosevelt. Again,
        you'll see a sign pointing ahead, along Roosevelt
        Avenue, to the Tomb of the Unknowns.

7.6   At a sign to the Tomb of the Unknowns pointing to
        the right onto a path, continue straight on Roosevelt
        Avenue. The hike goes to the tomb by a different
        route.

7.6-   You come to a fountain and balustrade on the left
        overlooking the lower part of the cemetery to the
        east. Opposite the fountain and balustrade are two
        parallel walkways leading west toward the Tomb of
        the Unknowns -- now visible at the top of a set of
        wide steps. Walk toward the tomb on the left-hand
        walkway.

7.6-   Before the walkway reaches the bottom of the set of
        wide steps, turn left (south) onto a smaller walkway.
        Continue on this walkway around to the right past
        two walkways intersecting from the left.

7.5   Arrive at the Tomb of the Unknowns.

        *An honor guard marches back and forth twenty-four
        hours a day, all year, in all weathers. The tomb
        contains the randomly selected, unidentified remains
        of one serviceman each from World War I, World War
        II, Korea, and Vietnam. Symbolizing a twenty-one gun
        salute, the guards march twenty-one steps and pause
        for twenty-one seconds. The elaborate changing of the
        guard at the tomb takes place every half hour from
        April through September and every hour for the
        remainder of the year. Members of the honor guard
        are stationed at Fort Myer, which you will visit later in
        this hike.*

7.5   To leave the tomb, walk up the steps directly to the
        west, across from the tomb, that lead to the columns
        of the white marble building. Walk around to the
        back of this building and then walk around the edge
        of the connected circular amphitheater. (See Map
        1-2.)

        *The entrance behind the columns of the white marble
        building leads to a small museum of military*

memorabilia. The amphitheater hosts the official services held each year on Memorial Day.

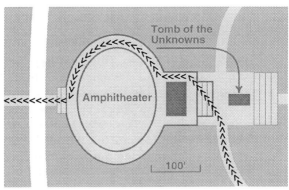

Map 1-2

7.4   Halfway around the amphitheater, descend a short flight of steps leaving the amphitheater , cross a road, and follow the walkway west toward the ship's mast. (See Map 1-2.)

7.4-   Arrive at the mast of the USS Maine.

The mast is from the battleship Maine, sunk by a mysterious explosion in Havana Harbor on February 15, 1898, with the loss of 260 American sailors. The sinking was an important incident leading to the Spanish-American War.

7.4-   Two roads lead north away from the mast of the battleship. Follow the one on your right.

7.3   At the first intersecting road, turn right. You are now on Farragut Avenue. (NOTE: There is a sign for Sigsbee Avenue at this intersection to designate the road leading away from the mast of the battleship, but the last time I was here, the sign rotated freely and was better indication of wind direction than of street orientation.)

Charles Dwight Sigsbee was captain of the Maine when it sank and a noted and innovative naval hydrographer. Admiral David Farragut led the Union Navy to a number of victories during the Civil War. He is perhaps most famous for the order he shouted at a critical and confused moment during the battle of Mobile Bay, "Damn the torpedoes! Full speed ahead!"

7.2   At the first intersection, turn sharply to the left. You are now on Wilson Avenue.

7.0   At the top of a hill, where Wilson Avenue intersects Meigs Avenue to the left, turn to the right around an equestrian statue of Philip Kearny, cross Sheridan Avenue, and then go straight onto a wide walkway called Lee Avenue. This walkway leads, first to the east and then to the north, to Arlington House. After visiting Arlington House, you must return by this same route to Meigs Avenue. (See Map 1-3.)

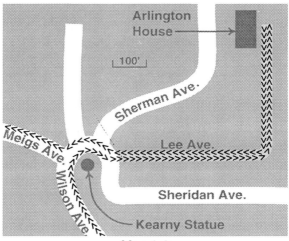

Map 1-3

Montgomery Meigs was Quartermaster General of the Union army and an unsung hero of Union victory. Philip Kearny was an aggressive Union brigadier who had lost an arm in the Mexican War. General Philip Sheridan was a highly successful Union cavalry officer. Robert E. Lee was, of course, the beloved commander of the Confederate Army of Northern Virginia.

Within the gardens to your left as you walk down Lee Avenue is the tomb of the unknown Civil War dead, containing the remains of 2,111 unidentified Union soldiers.

6.9   Arrive at the front of Arlington House. (See Map
        1-3.) There are public rest rooms and a drinking
        fountain behind the mansion at the back of the
        building containing the bookstore.

        A few steps in front of you as you look out over the city
        from the front of Arlington House is the grave of Pierre
        Charles L'Enfant, the tenacious and difficult
        Frenchman who laid out the original design for
        Washington.

        Arlington House was built by George Washington
        Parke Custis, grandson of Martha Washington and her
        first husband.   Custis was raised by George and
        Martha Washington at Mount Vernon.   Arlington
        House was completed in 1817.   Custis's daughter,
        Mary Anna, married Lieutenant Robert E. Lee at
        Arlington House two years after his graduation from
        West Point. The Lees made Arlington House their
        home until 1861, when General Lee left for Richmond
        to accept command of Virginia's military. The Lees
        never returned.   During the Civil War the House
        became a Union Army headquarters. Later it was used
        by the superintendent of the cemetery. Restoration of
        the house began in 1925, and in 1955 it was made a
        memorial to Lee.

6.8   Return to the intersection of Meigs and Wilson
        Avenues (at the Kearny statue) and walk west (away
        from the statue) on Meigs. (See Map 1-3.)

        A few steps down Meigs Avenue, on your right behind
        a large oak tree, is the grave of General Abner
        Doubleday, a hero of the battle of Gettysburg and the
        legendary inventor of baseball.

6.4   Pass through the gate in the red stone wall into Fort
        Myer and continue straight, past the chapel on your
        right, onto Lee Avenue. (See Map 1-4.)

        Fort Myer has served several functions through its
        history. The first military construction on the site was
        fortification works, named Fort Whipple, built in 1863
        as part of the Union defenses surrounding Washington
        during the Civil War. After the Civil War, the site was
        expanded, taken over by the Army Signal Corps, and

named after its commander, Colonel Albert James Myer. Colonel Myer is perhaps better known as the founder of the U.S. Weather Bureau. In 1887, under orders from Army Commanding General Philip Sheridan, Fort Myer was converted to a cavalry post. One of the Fort Myer's commanders during its days as a cavalry post was Colonel George S. Patton, Jr. In more recent years, the Fort is most noteworthy as the home of the Army Band (Pershing's Own) and the 1st Battalion, 3rd Infantry (the Old Guard), which performs ceremonial functions at Arlington National Cemetery and elsewhere around the nation's capital.

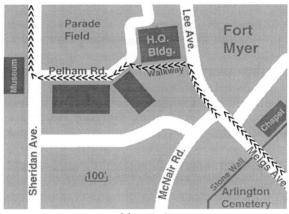

Map 1-4

6.3   Just before reaching the redbrick, white-balconied headquarters building on your left (the sign in front says "Headquarters Fort Myer"), turn left onto a walkway. At the rear of the headquarters building, where the walkway intersects a small street, turn left onto the street. This street becomes Pelham Road. (See Map 1-4.)

6.2   At the intersection of Pelham Road and Sheridan Avenue, cross and then turn right (north) onto Sheridan. (See Map 1-4.)

The small Old Guard Museum is across Sheridan Avenue at this intersection. The museum has a collection of Old Guard memorabilia, along with a small but fine collection of World War II infantry paintings.

The large parade field on your right as you walk down Sheridan Avenue played a part in early aviation history. In 1908 and 1909 the Wright Brothers flew their planes from this field to show their usefulness to the Army. The demonstrations led to a long-term Army contract for the Wrights.

6.0   Where Sheridan Avenue ends at its intersection with Jackson Avenue, cross and then turn right (east) onto Jackson.

Just north of the above intersection is the "Caisson" building that stables the ceremonial horses used by the Old Guard's Caisson Platoon. The horses pull the black caisson bearing the flag-draped casket in military funerals. The members of the Caisson Platoon are the last remaining official horsemen in the Army, a drastic comedown from the days when Fort Myer alone stabled more than fifteen hundred horses. The Caisson building is open to visitors from 12:00 noon to 4:00 pm.

5.8   Continue straight on Jackson Avenue as it winds downhill.

5.3   Pass through the Wright Gate, leaving Fort Myer, and, in a few steps, at the first intersecting road to the left, turn left onto Meade Street. Use the dirt path along the right side of Meade Street. You should now be walking toward the high-rise buildings of Rosslyn in the distance.

5.2   Just before reaching a small parking area on the right, turn onto a blacktop path that leads sharply to the right. This path leads to the United States Marine Corps War Memorial. (To continue the hike after visiting the Memorial, you must return to this point on Meade Street.)

5.1   Arrive at the Marine Corps Memorial.

The sculpture is based on a famous Pulitzer Prize-winning photograph of five Marines and one Navy hospital corpsman raising the flag over Mount Suribachi on Iwo Jima island on February 23, 1945.

> *Three of the Marines were later killed in the battle for Iwo Jima.*

5.0   Return to Meade Street and turn right (north), walking on the right side of the street, toward Rosslyn.

4.9   After crossing over a divided highway (Route 50), Meade Street divides into two large roads. At this point, follow the sidewalk around slightly to the right onto Lynn Street.

> *Rosslyn, a high-rise commercial area since the 1960s, has had a somewhat spotted history. Since the mid-18th century, Rosslyn has been a crossing point on the Potomac between Washington and Virginia, first by ferry, then by a canal boat aqueduct bridge (later also accommodating highway and rail traffic), and, finally, by the current Francis Scott Key Bridge. During the late 19th and early 20th centuries, Rosslyn was notorious for its saloons and gambling houses. After these dens of iniquity had been eliminated, Rosslyn became a center for pawn shops, usury laws being less strict in Virginia than in Washington.*

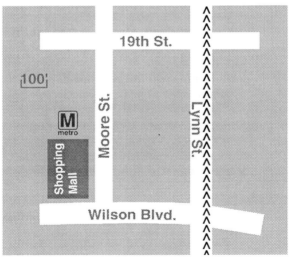

Map 1-5

4.7   At the intersection of Lynn Street and Wilson Boulevard, cross Wilson and continue straight on Lynn. The Rosslyn Metro station and the shopping mall (with the delicatessen and a number of carry-

out restaurants) are located on Moore Street (the
parallel street one block to the left of Lynn Street)
between Wilson Boulevard and 19th Street. (See
Map 1-5.)

4.5   North Lynn Street crosses Lee Highway right-bound,
        then passes over a divided highway (Interstate Route
        66), and then crosses Lee Highway left-bound.
        Immediately after crossing left-bound Lee Highway,
        turn right onto a blacktop path. (The hike returns to
        this point in 2.4 miles after you explore Theodore
        Roosevelt Island.)

4.3   Cross over a divided highway (George Washington
        Memorial Parkway) on a concrete foot/bicycle
        bridge and then follow the path south down the
        western bank of the Potomac. As you walk here, the
        river should be on your left.

        *The river here is a channel of the Potomac between
        Virginia and Theodore Roosevelt Island. The main
        channel of the Potomac flows between the island and
        Washington.*

4:1   After passing a parking area, turn left and cross the
        one-lane bridge to Theodore Roosevelt Island.

        *The view of Key Bridge to the left as you cross the
        bridge is a favorite subject for landscape artists.*

4.0   On reaching the island, you come to an information
        board where brochures about the island are normally
        available. (You will eventually return to this point
        and leave the island by the same bridge.) To
        continue the hike on the island, turn right at the
        information board onto the wide gravel trail and
        follow the trail around to the left. (See Map 1-6.)

3.9   Arrive at the Theodore Roosevelt Memorial. (See
        Map 1-6.) (NOTE: You should return to this point
        to leave the Memorial.) The Memorial is an
        excellent place for a picnic; if you prefer more
        seclusion, there are benches later in the hike along
        the trail around the island.

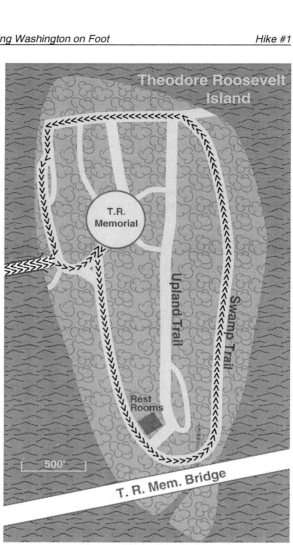

Map 1-6

The 88-acre island originally was known by its Indian name -- Analostan Island. It passed through various European owners and names until, in 1717, it was purchased by the father of George Mason, Virginia statesman and delegate to the Constitutional Convention. George Mason's son, John, converted the island to a farm estate, building a large brick house, the foundations of which are still visible. After more than a century, the Mason family was forced to abandon the island because of the stench and unhealthy conditions created by stagnant water collected behind a causeway built between the island and the Virginia shore. The causeway was built to force all the river's current into the silted main channel in an attempt to maintain its navigability. Later owners developed the island for recreation and sports. In 1932 the island was purchased by the Theodore Roosevelt Memorial Association as a gift to the American people to commemorate the conservationist president. A formal memorial was built on the island in spite of considerable opposition from those who believed that the most appropriate memorial was an undeveloped wilderness.

3.9-   After leaving the Memorial, turn left at the first branch in the trail. You are now on a wide trail going south on the island. (See Map 1-6.)

3.6   Come to public rest rooms with a drinking fountain. Immediately past the rest rooms, the trail divides, with the Swamp Trail leading to the right and the Upland Trail leading to the left. Take the Swamp Trail to the right.

        (NOTE: The Swamp Trail, while scenic and interesting, is sometimes flooded and almost always muddy. Also, in summer, patches of poison ivy and stinging nettles grow along the route. You can avoid the mud and irritating plants by taking the Upland Trail which rejoins the Swamp Trail at 3.0- below. To follow the Upland Trail, ascend a short rise behind the rest rooms, turn left, walk relatively straight for about 0.3 miles, and then turn left where the Upland Trail ends at its re-connection with the Swamp Trail. After making this turn, continue the hike starting with the direction given at 2.9 below. Both the Upland and the Swamp Trail are shown in Map 1-6.)

3.5   A short distance down the Swamp Trail, you come to a pier of the Theodore Roosevelt Memorial Bridge. Bear to the left, leaving the pier on your right, and in a few steps cross a wooden footbridge. (See Map 1-6.) At this point there is a beautiful small marsh to your left.

3.5-   After crossing the footbridge, bear to the left. The marsh should now be on your left. The main channel of the Potomac is a short distance to your right, just visible through the trees. (See Map 1-6.)

3.1   The trail ascends a short rise and turns gradually to the left.

3.0   Where the trail intersects another large trail that leads down to the river to your right, turn left. (See Map 1-6.) You may want to take a short detour to the river bank down the trail to the right. Here you will get a panoramic view across the river of the Georgetown waterfront, part of which you will visit later in the hike.

3.0-   In a few steps, continue straight where the Upland Trail intersects perpendicularly from the left. (See Map 1-6.)

2.9   At a drinking fountain, where a large trail intersects from the left, continue straight. (See Map 1-6.)

2.9-   In a short distance, where a smaller trail intersects from the left, continue straight down toward the bank of the river. (See Map 1-6.)

2.8   A few steps before reaching the river bank, turn left. As you walk here, the river should be immediately to your right. (See Map 1-6.)

2.8-   In a short distance, where the trail divides, bear to the right. (See Map 1-6.)

2.6   At the information board, turn right and return to the mainland via the bridge. (See Map 1-6.)

2.5   At the mainland side of the bridge, turn right and follow the trail back north along the river.

2.3   Ascend the concrete ramp leading to the foot/bicycle bridge over the George Washington Memorial Parkway.

2.1   Return to the point where North Lynn Street crosses Lee Highway westbound. Turn right here and follow the sidewalk onto Key Bridge, crossing over the Potomac from Rosslyn to Georgetown.

From the bridge you can see Theodore Roosevelt Island down-river to your right, close to the Virginia shore. Across the main channel of the river from the island, on the Washington shore, is the historic Georgetown waterfront. The stone towers on the hill to the left of the bridge are part of Georgetown University.

(CAUTION: Two-thirds of the way across the bridge, you must cross an exit ramp where cars coming from behind you turn right off the bridge, at high speed.)

1.8   At the far end of the bridge, follow the sidewalk around to the right (east) onto M Street.

The small park to your right, flying the U.S. flag of the War of 1812 (fifteen stars and fifteen stripes), is Francis Scott Key Park.

1.7   In one short block, at the intersection of M and 34th Streets, cross M Street and come back along M on the other side in the opposite direction (west).

The stone-and-redbrick building just west of 35th Street is called the Car Barn and until 1950 served as a streetcar barn. The building, constructed in the late 1890s, was originally designed to serve as a union station, connecting what were then separately owned streetcar lines: the Washington and Georgetown line along M St. (a cable car line at the time), the Metropolitan Railroad line along Prospect Street at roof level behind the building, and two lines from Virginia. As this was well before the construction of Key Bridge, the Virginia lines crossed the Potomac on a superstructure built over the old Aqueduct Bridge that connected the Chesapeake and Ohio Canal on the D.C. side of the river with the Alexandria Canal on the Virginia side.

1.6   Immediately after passing the Car Barn, make a turn to the right, walk along the west side of the Car Barn, and then climb the narrow and imposing seventy-five steps made infamous by the movie "The Exorcist."

1.5   At the top of the steps, turn right (east) onto Prospect
       Street.

       Straight (north) up 36th Street a short distance is a
       basement restaurant on the left that is open during
       the day and is a good place to rest after the arduous
       climb and get a drink and a snack.

       *A few steps down Prospect Street is the original roof
       level entrance to the Car Barn. To your rear, west
       down Prospect Street, once ran the streetcar line that
       connected the city to the popular amusement park at
       Glen Echo, Maryland. The last streetcar lines running
       in Washington were abandoned in 1962.*

1.3   After walking east a few blocks on Prospect Street,
       turn right (south) onto Potomac Street.

1.2   In one block, at the intersection of Potomac and M
       Streets, cross M and come to the old, redbrick
       Georgetown Market. The sign on the market
       building now reads "Dean & Deluca." (See Map
       1-7.)

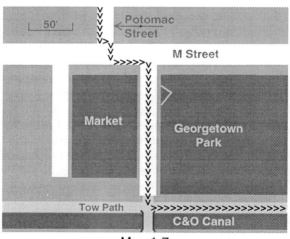

Map 1-7

*Built in 1865, the Georgetown Market was one of
Washington's many farmers markets. It has been
refurbished into a modern grocers and restaurant and
is another good place to stop.*

1.2   To continue the hike, walk down the small,
       pedestrian side street perpendicular to M Street, on

the left (east) side of the market building. (See Map 1-7.)

A few steps down this side street, on the left, is an entrance to the Georgetown Park shopping mall, where you can find restaurants and public rest rooms.

1.2-   Past the end of the market building, you come to some steps leading down to a footbridge over the Chesapeake and Ohio (C&O) canal. Walk down the steps, but do not cross the bridge. Instead, walk down another short set of steps to the left leading to the canal towpath. Follow the towpath to the east. The canal should be to your right as you walk along the towpath. (See Map 1-7.)

The building to your left, presently containing the shopping mall, was once a streetcar repair shop. The building to your right, across the canal, produced electric power for the streetcar system.

The C&O Canal connected Georgetown and its tidewater harbor to Cumberland, Maryland, 183 miles behind you to the west. In front of you the canal drops 32 feet, through four locks, and then, about a mile ahead, ends at a tide lock where it connects with the Potomac River. To travel the entire length of the canal a boat would pass through 74 locks and would be raised or lowered 610 feet. During the warmer months, the U.S. Park Service now operates a mule-drawn canal boat along the stretch of the canal in Georgetown. With boatmen and women in period costume, the boat is authentic in every respect except that its hull is made of concrete. If you are lucky, you will see the boat in operation as it ascends and descends through the locks. But don't stand around too long or you may be asked to help open or close one of the lock gates.

Through the first half of this century this part of Georgetown (between the canal and the river a block to your right) was very industrial and had none too good a reputation or smell. Now it is the location of some of the most exclusive residences, offices, restaurants, and shops in the city.

0.9   Where the tow path crosses Thomas Jefferson Street, turn right (south) onto Thomas Jefferson and cross over the canal.

0.8   In one block, where Thomas Jefferson Street intersects K Street, continue straight (south) across K, under the elevated highway, onto a wide walkway between two sand-colored brick buildings.

The buildings make up the architecturally unusual -- some might say strange -- Washington Harbour complex, one of the more spectacular and controversial improvements on the Georgetown waterfront. As you pass between the buildings, don't feel too silly if you find yourself smiling at, or courteously moving aside for, one of the casually placed, unusually realistic sculptures of visitors and workmen. Everyone is fooled and then delighted.

0.7   On the opposite side of a large pool and fountains is a boardwalk along the Potomac. Turn left onto the boardwalk. As you walk along the boardwalk, the river should be to your right.

Theodore Roosevelt Island is across the river from the boardwalk.

0.6   At the end of the boardwalk, continue in the same direction a short distance along the bank of the river, across an area that is presently in a confused and unpaved state of development.

0.6-   Before reaching a boat house (Thompson's Boat Center), turn left onto the paved road and, in a short distance, cross over Rock Creek on a narrow highway bridge.

At this point, Rock Creek also served as the C&O Canal, which merges with the creek a quarter mile upstream to your left. To your right, downstream, are the remains of the tide lock that maintained a constant level in the canal/creek where it entered the tidal Potomac. Just upstream of the tide lock was the beginning of a short canal that led down the bank of the Potomac and then inland along Constitution

Avenue where canal boats could connect with the Washington City Canal.

0.5   A short distance farther on, cross the divided Rock Creek Parkway and continue straight (southwest) up the right side of Virginia Avenue.

Along this stretch of Virginia Avenue you pass between the Watergate complex and the Howard Johnson Motor Lodge made famous by the Watergate scandal. The Democratic National Campaign headquarters were in the Watergate office building on your right. The Watergate burglars had lookouts stationed in rooms across the street in the Howard Johnson's. The break-in of the Democratic headquarters occurred in the early morning of June 17, 1972, and the scandal led eventually to Nixon's resignation as president on August 9, 1974.

There are restaurants and public rest rooms (the last before the end of the hike) in a small shopping mall in the lower level of the third Watergate building on your right.

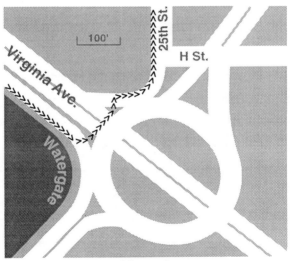

Map 1-8

0.3   Where the Watergate complex ends, turn left and cross Virginia Avenue at a traffic light, and then go north on 25th Street. (See Map 1-8.)

Since leaving the Potomac River and until the end of the hike, you are passing through the Foggy Bottom neighborhood. Once a center of small industry located in the foggy lowlands along the river and the canal, Foggy Bottom is now one of the most exclusive residential areas of the city. Its name is sometimes used by journalists as a synonym for the State Department located several blocks away. The small, quaint, restored row houses along 25th Street and I Street were once very modest workers' dwellings, and the streets and alleys were once crowded with workers' children.

0.2   In one block, at the intersection of 25th and I Streets, turn right (east) onto I.

0.1   In one block, after crossing New Hampshire Avenue and then 24th Street, I Street becomes a small park. Continue east through this park.

0.0   At the other end of the park, at the intersection of I and 23rd Streets, is the entrance to the Foggy Bottom Metro station and the end of the hike.

NOTES

_____

_____

_____

_____

_____

_____

_____

_____

_____

_____

_____

_____

_____

_____

_____

_____

_____

_____

_____

_____

_____

_____

_____

_____

_____

_____

_____

_____

_____

_____

_____

_____

_____

_____

_____

_____

_____

_____

_____

_____

_____

_____

_____

_____

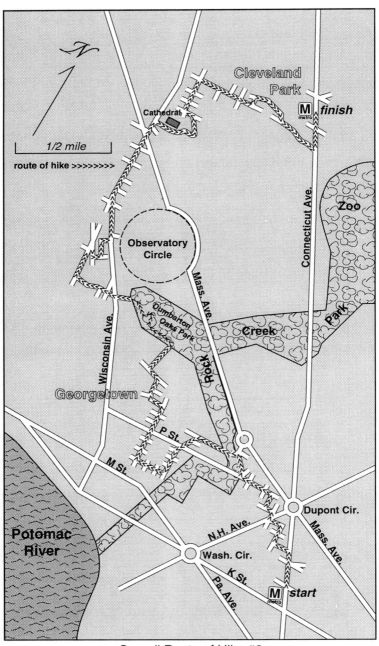

Overall Route of Hike #2
Farragut North to Cleveland Park

HIKE #2

A grand old neighborhood; a restored colonial town and its African American roots; a short walk through a secluded woods; a Cold War relic; a magnificent cathedral; and mansions in an old in-town suburb.

From: Farragut North Metro Station (D.C.)

To: Cleveland Park Metro Station (D.C.)

Via: Connecticut Avenue, P Street, east Georgetown, Dumbarton Oaks Park, Glover Park, Wisconsin Avenue, Washington National Cathedral, and Cleveland Park.

Distance: 6.1 miles

Duration: 3 hours if you walk at 2.5 miles per hour and make two 10-minute and one 15-minute stops.

Highlights

From the Farragut North Metro station, you will walk north up busy, commercial Connecticut Avenue and then west, along quieter streets, past some of what remains of the once grand and elegant Dupont Circle area. After crossing over Rock Creek Park on the Dumbarton (Q Street) Bridge, you will enter the eastern end of Georgetown, with its fashionable restored 18th- and 19th-century row houses and mansions. But first, the hike takes you through a cluster of humbler dwellings, known as Herring Hill, a tiny neighborhood that was once home to African American servants who worked in the big houses to the west. Then you will move north out of Georgetown, past the magnificent formal gardens of Dumbarton Oaks, down Lovers' Lane, and into the small, secluded, almost secret woods of Dumbarton Oaks Park. Emerging from the park, you will cross Wisconsin Avenue and enter a quaint neighborhood of newer and less grand town houses known as Glover Park. From Glover Park you will hike uphill on Wisconsin Avenue, past the fortress-like Russian (previously Soviet) embassy compound, and arrive at the magnificent Washington National Cathedral. The hike takes you through the cathedral close, past the towering

Gothic cathedral and the lovely Bishop's Garden. After leaving the close, you will walk through Cleveland Park, an early suburb of large detached houses, including some fanciful architectural gems. From here you will return to Connecticut Avenue, far to the north of where you started, and end the hike at the Cleveland Park Metro Station.

Things to Know Before You Start

All distances shown in parentheses below indicate miles to the end of the hike.

Intermediate Metro Stations

There are no convenient Metro Stations along the route of this hike.

Places to Stop for a Rest

Convenient rest stops along the route of this hike are: a small park at the intersection of 23rd and Q Streets (5.1 miles), Mount Zion Cemetery (4.8 miles), Montrose Park (3.8 miles), Dumbarton Oaks Park (3.4 miles), and the Bishops Garden (1.5 miles).

Places to Stop and Eat

There are several restaurants and carry-outs along P Street between 20th and 22nd Streets (5.4 miles). If you are in the mood for a picnic, this is a good place to get provisions. Fine picnic spots include Mount Zion Cemetery (4.8 miles), Montrose Park (3.8 miles), and Dumbarton Oaks Park (3.4 miles). There is another cluster of restaurants along Wisconsin Avenue north of Hall Place (2.3 miles). Last, and most important, you'll find abundant restaurants at the end of the hike along Connecticut Avenue.

Public Rest Rooms

Accessible rest rooms are located at Montrose Park (3.8 miles) and the Washington National Cathedral (1.6 miles).

Some Cautions

For a short distance, in Dumbarton Oaks Park, the hike follows a narrow dirt trail. This trail can be muddy and slippery when wet. Also, in late summer, the trail tends to be overgrown with vegetation that may include poison ivy.

On-Route Directions After You Start

Numbers in the left margin indicate miles to the end of the hike. Unless otherwise indicated, maps are oriented north to top of page.

6.1   There are three exits from the Farragut North Metro station, one leading to K Street and two to L Street. After you alight from the train, walk along the train platform in the direction of the arrows pointing to L Street to the escalators at the end of the platform. On reaching street level, at the northeast corner of L Street and Connecticut Avenue, turn right and cross Connecticut. On the other side, turn right and walk north on the avenue.

Connecticut Avenue is one of the city's grand boulevards. The intersection of Connecticut Avenue and K Street, one block behind you, is considered the center of Washington's downtown office district, where lobbyists, lawyers, stock brokers, and the like do business and entertain clients. The avenue in the direction you are walking leads in a few blocks to Dupont Circle, the center of the city's most opulent residential neighborhood around the turn of the century. Today this part of Connecticut Avenue is known for its retail shops and restaurants.

As you walk up the first block of Connecticut Avenue, look to your right up the next intersecting street and you will see the red-stone-and-brick Saint Matthew's Cathedral. The Roman Catholic cathedral was completed in 1899 and has been the site of many important religious events, including a mass performed by Pope John Paul II during his 1979 visit to Washington. It is probably best known, however, as the site of John F. Kennedy's funeral service in 1963.

6.0   At the end of the first block, where Connecticut
        Avenue intersects M Street, cross M and continue
        north on Connecticut. There is a tiny triangular park
        here with a drinking fountain and a statue of the poet
        Henry Wadsworth Longfellow. At the end of this
        park, cross 18th Street and then turn left (west) onto
        Jefferson Place.

5.8   In one block, at the intersection of Jefferson Place
        and 19th Street, turn right (north) onto 19th.

5.7   In two short blocks, at the intersection of 19th Street
        and Sunderland Place, turn left (west) onto
        Sunderland.

        On the right (north) side of Sunderland Place,
        beginning about mid-block and continuing to the next
        intersection, are the grounds of the Christian Heurich
        Mansion -- one of the few reminders of past opulence
        in the Dupont Circle neighborhood. The classic
        Victorian mansion was built between 1892 and 1894
        as the home of Washington's most prominent brewer.
        Heurich's original brewery was located a short
        distance south on 20th Street. He later built a larger
        brewery in Foggy Bottom. This last brewery was torn
        down in 1966 to make room for the Kennedy Center
        and adjacent highways. In keeping with the owner's
        profession, the mansion includes an authentic
        rathskeller. Scheduled tours of the mansion are
        provided by its present owners, the Historical Society
        of Washington.

5.6   At the end of the block, at the intersection of
        Sunderland Place, 20th Street, and New Hampshire
        Avenue, cross 20th and then turn right (north) and
        cross New Hampshire. You should now be walking
        north on 20th Street.

5.6-   In one short block, at the intersection of 20th and O
        Streets, turn left (west) onto O.

5.5   In one block, at the intersection of O and Hopkins
        Streets, turn right (north) onto Hopkins.

5.4   In one block, at the intersection of Hopkins and P
        Streets, turn left (west) onto P. You'll pass many

restaurants and carry-outs in the next two blocks on P Street.

Now one of the centers of gay life in the city, this stretch of P Street retains some of the Bohemian reputation that much of the Dupont Circle neighborhood had during the 1960s when it was a gathering place for hippies, war protesters, and civil rights activists.

5.2   One short block after crossing 22nd Street, at the intersection of P and 23rd Streets, cross 23rd, then turn right (north) across P, and follow 23rd north. After a few steps, follow 23rd Street (unmarked) as it curves to the left along the edge of Rock Creek Park. (See Map 2-1.)

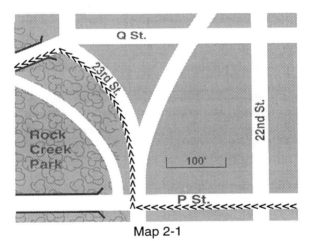

Map 2-1

5.1   In one block, at the intersection of 23rd and Q Streets, turn left onto Q and cross over Rock Creek Park on the Dumbarton Bridge to Georgetown. (See Map 2-1.) Before crossing the bridge, you may want to stop and rest in the beautiful shaded little park on the southeast corner of 23rd and Q Streets.

4.9   One long block after crossing the Dumbarton Bridge, Q Street intersects 27th Street to your left (south) and the narrow Mill Street to your right (north). Turn right here onto Mill Street. (When I last walked this hike, there were no street signs for 27th or Mill Streets at this intersection).

A short distance down Mill Street, you come to the secluded and historic Mount Zion Cemetery, founded in 1879. Seemingly out of place in the affluent and nearly all-white neighborhood of today, the cemetery was once part of a large African American community located at eastern edge of Georgetown in a neighborhood called Herring Hill (named after the fish taken from nearby Rock Creek). Many of its residents worked as servants in the white homes to the west. With the gentrification of Georgetown that began in the 1930s, blacks were mostly displaced by affluent whites, and all that remains of the Herring Hill community are a few churches still lovingly maintained by African American parishioners now scattered around the metropolitan area.

4.8   After visiting Mount Zion Cemetery, retrace your steps back along Mill Street.

4.7   On returning to the intersection of Mill, Q, and 27th Streets, cross Q and go straight (south) down 27th.

As you walk down 27th Street you pass through the heart of Herring Hill. The First Baptist Church (founded in 1862) on the southeast corner of 27th and Dumbarton Streets is one of the original Herring Hill churches.

4.4   At the intersection of 27th and N Streets, turn right (west) onto N.

The house at 2812 N Street was the residence of Susan Decatur, the young widow of Stephen Decatur -- U.S. naval hero during the War of 1812 and famous for his words: "Our country . . . may she always be right; but our country, right or wrong." The Decaturs lived in a large house on Lafayette Square until Stephen's death in a duel in 1820 forced Susan to relocate to this "smaller" house in Georgetown.

4.2   In three blocks, at the intersection of N and 30th Streets, turn right (north) onto 30th.

4.0   One short block after crossing Q Street, at the intersection of 30th and Cambridge Place, turn left (west) onto Cambridge.

3.9   In one block, where Cambridge Place ends, turn
       right (north) onto Avon Place. (The last time I
       passed here, there were no street signs at this
       intersection.)

3.8   Where Avon Place ends at its intersection with R
       Street, cross and then turn left onto R. Montrose
       Park is on the right (north) side of R Street here. The
       park has drinking fountains, rest rooms, benches, and
       picnic tables and is a good place to rest and picnic.

3.7   In a short block, at the end of Montrose Park, is a
       small lane leading off to the right (north) separating
       the park from the walled grounds of Dumbarton
       Oaks. This is Lovers' Lane, which had no street sign
       the last time I walked this way. To continue the
       hike, turn right (north) onto Lovers' Lane. An iron
       pipe gate normally blocks Lovers' Lane to vehicular
       traffic.

       *If you have time (a minimum of one hour), you may
       want to detour and visit the magnificent formal
       gardens of Dumbarton Oaks. To reach the entrance of
       Dumbarton Oaks, continue west on R Street half a
       block past Lovers' Lane.*

3.5   At the bottom of a hill on Lovers' Lane, where the
       pavement on the lane ends and a wooded area
       begins, turn left onto the dirt path that follows the
       wall of Dumbarton Oaks through a gate. As you
       walk here, you should see a small stream to your
       right. (See Map 2-2.)

3.5-   In a short distance, cross the stream on a stone bridge
       and continue on the path as it bears to the left on the
       other side. (See Map 2-2.) The stream should now
       be on your left and a small hillside meadow on your
       right.

       *The stream is a tributary of Rock Creek, and the quiet,
       secluded, woodland and meadow surrounding you is
       the pocket-size (27-acre) wilderness of Dumbarton
       Oaks Park. The formal gardens of Dumbarton Oaks
       are adjacent to the park but not accessible from this
       direction.*

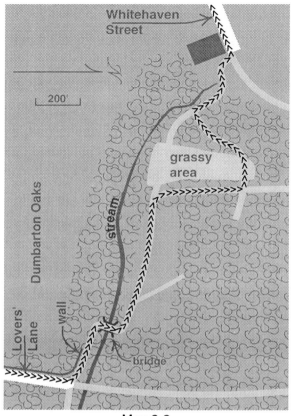

Map 2-2

3.4   Continue along the stream (to your left) for about
       100 yards and then, just before reaching a mowed
       grassy area, follow the trail as it turns to the right
       and leads uphill, away from the stream. (See Map
       2-2.)

3.3   In a short distance, at the intersection with a smaller
       dirt trail, turn left onto the smaller trail. In a few
       steps, cross the top edge of the grassy area and
       continue on the trail into the woods on the other side.
       (See Map 2-2.)

3.2   In a short distance, down a hill, where the trail ends
       at its intersection with another dirt trail, turn right
       onto the other trail. (See Map 2-2.) The stream
       should now be on your left again.

3.1   After ascending a steep hill and passing along the side of a redbrick building, the trail leaves the park and comes to Whitehaven Street. Turn left (west) and follow the sidewalk along the left side of Whitehaven. (See Map 2-2.)

3.0   Where Whitehaven Street intersects Wisconsin Avenue, cross Wisconsin on the crosswalk a little to the left down the avenue, and continue in the same direction (west) on Whitehaven Parkway.

2.8   At the intersection of Whitehaven Parkway and 37th Street, turn right (north) onto 37th. There is a park with picnic tables across 37th Street.

2.6   At the intersection of 37th Street and Tunlaw Road, turn sharply to the right (southeast) onto Tunlaw.

2.5   At the next intersection, turn left onto W Place. (When I was last here, there was no street sign for W Place.)

2.4   In one block, at the intersection of W Place and Hall Place, turn left (north) onto Hall.

2.4-   Follow Hall Place as it turns to the right (east).

2.3   Where Hall Place ends at Wisconsin Avenue, turn left (north) onto Wisconsin. In the next block of Wisconsin Avenue, there are several restaurants and carry-out food shops.

          On the left (west) side of Wisconsin Avenue, a short distance past (north of) Calvert Street, is the large Russian Embassy compound. The property was acquired and developed during the active spying days of the Soviet Union. Allowing the Soviets to locate here was considered by many to be a major U.S. intelligence blunder, since this is one of the highest points in Washington and presumably an excellent location for electronic surveillance of the city.

1.8   After following Wisconsin Avenue up a long rise, cross the avenue at its intersection with Garfield Street, and continue in the same direction (north) on

the other side. There is a small park on your right
here with benches and a drinking fountain.

1.7   At the intersection of Wisconsin and Massachusetts
       Avenues, cross Massachusetts and continue in the
       same direction (north) on Wisconsin.

1.6   Half a block after crossing Massachusetts Avenue,
       just after passing the small Saint Albans Church on
       your right, turn right (east) onto the roadway leading
       into the grounds -- the "close" -- of the Washington
       National Cathedral. To continue the hike, follow
       this roadway along the right side of the cathedral.
       (See Map 2-3.) You can visit the cathedral by
       entering through the doors facing Wisconsin
       Avenue. There are rest rooms and drinking water in
       the cathedral.

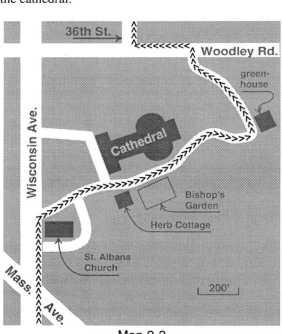

Map 2-3

Construction on the cathedral, officially named the
Cathedral Church of Saint Peter and Saint Paul,
began in 1907 and was not completed until 1990. It is
the sixth largest cathedral in the world and is probably
the last pure Gothic work of construction in the world.
Like other cathedrals, it is built in the shape of a
Christian cross.   The entrance facing Wisconsin
Avenue, the center portal, is at the foot of the cross.

Funeral services for presidents, members of Congress, and leading military officers have been held here. Dr. Martin Luther King Jr., gave his last sermon in the cathedral less than a week before his assassination. Woodrow Wilson, Helen Keller and her teacher, Annie Sullivan, are entombed here. There is also a story that one of the cathedral stone masons, not being allowed to inter his wife's remains in the building, mixed her ashes with some mortar that was used in its construction.

1.5   On the right side of the road that runs past the cathedral is an arched doorway in a wall leading to the small, exquisite Bishop's Garden. This is an ideal place to rest and, if you are so inclined, to meditate. (See Map 2-3.)

1.4   After following the road past the cathedral, just before reaching the greenhouse, follow the road as it turns sharply to the left. (See Map 2-3.)

1.3   After passing through a gate of the cathedral close, cross the public street, Woodley Road, and turn to the left (west). (See Map 2-3.)

1.2   In half a block, at the intersection of Woodley Road and 36th Street, turn right (north) onto 36th.

From here to the end of the hike you will pass through the neighborhood of Cleveland Park. Most of the houses here were built in the late nineteenth and early twentieth centuries as part of an organized real estate development made possible by the extension of Connecticut Avenue past Rock Creek in 1891 and the opening of streetcar service on both Connecticut and Wisconsin Avenues. Cleveland Park offered well-off professionals a quiet place to live away from the noisy, hot, congested city. The real estate developers encouraged diverse, one-of-a-kind houses designed by local architects. The success of their efforts remains apparent today. During the 1930s and 40s the neighborhood dropped out of fashion and many of the grand old houses became rundown. Some were divided up to satisfy the World War II housing demand. Since the 1960s, however, Cleveland Park has regained its original affluent, small-town character and it is now one of the most sought-after neighborhoods in the city.

On the southeast corner of 36th and Newark Streets stood Oak View -- a large stone house built in 1869. In 1885 President Grover Cleveland purchased the house as a summer home for his new wife and himself. Cleveland had the house remodeled into a fanciful Victorian dwelling and it served as the summer White House through his first term in office. It is from President Cleveland's residence here that the neighborhood takes its name.

1.0   In three blocks, at the intersection of 36th and Newark Streets, turn right (east) onto Newark.

The large frame farm house set well back from the street to your left a short distance down Newark Street was the center of a large 18th-century estate known as Rosedale. The house itself was built in 1794. One of the founders of Rosedale was General Uriah Forrest -- formerly the mayor of Georgetown and George Washington's aide-de-camp in the Revolutionary War. During the 19th century the estate was gradually subdivided, and part of it eventually became the site of Cleveland Park and National Cathedral.

0.7   One block after the intersection of Newark and 34th Streets, turn left (north) onto 33rd Place.

0.7- In one block, turn right (east) onto Highland Place. (The last time I was here, there was no street sign for Highland Place.)

0.5   At the intersection of Highland Place and Newark Street, turn left (east) onto Newark.

0.2   At the intersection of Newark Street and Connecticut Avenue, turn left (north) onto Connecticut.

0.0   Half a block after crossing Ordway Street, you reach the Cleveland Park Metro station entrance and the end of this hike. However, you may want to stop at one of the many restaurants that line both sides of Connecticut Avenue in the two blocks north of Newark Street.

NOTES

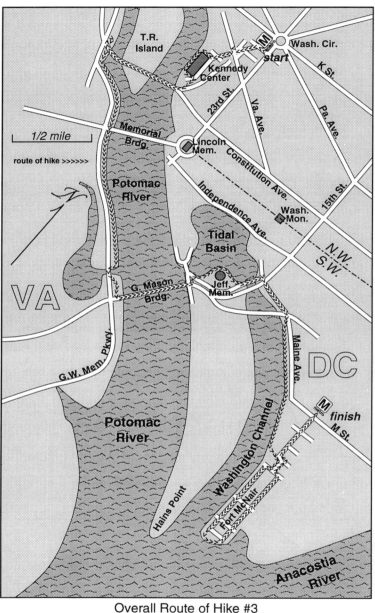

Overall Route of Hike #3
Foggy Bottom to Waterfront

HIKE #3

A working-class town turned into charming row houses and a performing arts center; a walk down the river bank with monumental views of the city; a floating seafood market; a boat-filled waterfront; and a haunted army post.

From: Foggy Bottom Metro Station (D.C.)

To: Waterfront Metro Station (D.C.)

Via: The Foggy Bottom neighborhood, the John F. Kennedy Center for the Performing Arts, Theodore Roosevelt Bridge, the Virginia bank of the Potomac River, the George Mason Bridge, the Tidal Basin, the Jefferson Memorial, the Washington Waterfront, and Fort McNair.

Distance: 7.6 miles

Duration: 3 hours 30 minutes if you walk at 2.5 miles per hour and make three 10-minute stops.

Highlights

From the Foggy Bottom Metro station, you will walk past the small, quaint, restored row houses of Foggy Bottom and then around the concourse of the John F. Kennedy Center for the Performing Arts with its beautiful riverbank view of the Potomac. From the Kennedy Center you will cross the river, from D.C. to Virginia, on Theodore Roosevelt Bridge and pass over the forest, marshes, and abundant water birds on Theodore Roosevelt Island. The hike then takes you down the Virginia bank of the Potomac, giving you magnificent cross-river views of the monumental city. After crossing back over the river to D.C. on the George Mason (Fourteenth Street) Bridge, you will walk along the cherry-tree-lined edge of the Tidal Basin past the Jefferson Memorial. From the Tidal Basin, the hike leads you along the Washington waterfront, past the floating seafood market and a variety of yachts and waterside restaurants. Next you will arrive at the ordered seclusion of Fort McNair, where the Lincoln assassination conspirators were hanged and buried. Here are more wonderful views of the river. From Fort McNair, you will walk a short distance past new and old houses in the Southwest redevelopment area and end the hike at the Waterfront Metro station.

Things to Know Before You Start

All distances in parentheses below indicate miles to the end of the hike.

Intermediate Metro Stations

There are no convenient Metro stations located along the route of this hike.

Places to Stop for a Rest

Convenient rest stops along the route are: the terrace of the Kennedy Center (7.2 miles), the Virginia bank of the Potomac (6.0 to 4.4 miles), the Jefferson Memorial (3.5 miles), the southern end of the waterfront (2.3 miles), and the southern end of Fort McNair (1.2 miles).

Places to Stop and Eat

The best place to eat is at the string of restaurants along the Washington Waterfront (2.8 to 2.3 miles). These same restaurants are also a short walk from the Waterfront Metro station at the end of the hike (0.0 miles). There is a fast-food restaurant with pleasant outdoor seating at the Columbia Island Motor Boat Marina (4.7 miles) and a few small restaurants at Waterside Mall at the end of the hike (0.0 miles). During warm weather, you can usually get fresh steamed crabs and other seafood at the Washington seafood market (2.9 miles) and eat at one of the few outdoor tables available there. If you would prefer to picnic, there are many good, shaded, grassy spots along the Virginia bank of the Potomac (6.0 to 4.4 miles).

Public Rest Rooms

Public rest rooms are located along the route at: the Kennedy Center (7.1 miles), though the building may not be open when you are in need; the Columbia Island Motor Boat Marina (4.7

miles); the Jefferson Memorial (3.5 miles); the Washington seafood market (2.9 miles); and Waterside Mall (0.0 miles).

On-Route Directions After You Start

Numbers in the left margin indicate miles to the end of the hike. Unless otherwise indicated, maps are oriented north to top of page.

7.6   There is only one exit from the Foggy Bottom Metro station. On reaching street level from the Metro Station, make a U-turn to the right and walk west through a small linear park that takes the place of I Street between 23rd and 24th Streets.

7.5   At the end of the park, at the intersection of 24th and I Streets, cross 24th and continue straight (west) on I.

7.5-   In a few steps, at the intersection of I Street and New Hampshire Avenue, cross and then turn half left (southwest) onto New Hampshire.

The string of small, quaint, restored row houses on the right side of New Hampshire Avenue, now the homes of middle-class professionals, once housed working class families who gained their livelihood from a strip of industries located primarily on the low, sometimes foggy bottom land a short distance to your right along the Potomac River. One of the ugliest installations in the neighborhood was a gas works, which stored its output in two huge tanks located on the left side of New Hampshire Avenue just past H Street. The removal of these storage tanks in the 1950s opened the way for the restoration of the neighborhood.

7.4   In one block, at the intersection of New Hampshire Avenue and H Street, continue straight across H to a traffic island. (See Map 3-1.)

7.4-   In a few steps, at the far end of the traffic island, turn right and leave the traffic island by crossing the street to your right on a crosswalk. (See Map 3-1.)

7.4-   After crossing the street from the traffic island, turn left and then, in a few steps, turn left again onto a crosswalk to another, smaller traffic island. From

this traffic island continue straight across the divided
Virginia Avenue. (See Map 3-1.)

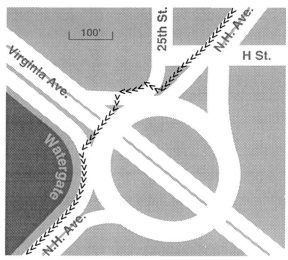

Map 3-1

7.3   On the other side of Virginia Avenue, after crossing
        over another small traffic island, turn left and follow
        the sidewalk as it turns gradually to the right, past
        the curve of the Watergate Building, back onto New
        Hampshire Avenue. (The last time I passed here,
        there was no sign for New Hampshire Avenue.) As
        you continue (southwest) down New Hampshire, the
        Watergate buildings should be on your right. (See
        Map 3-1.)

        *Although it will forever be associated with political
        scandal, the name Watergate has more tranquil
        origins. "Water Gate" was originally the name given
        to a wide set of marble steps, a short distance to the
        south next to Memorial Bridge, that form an
        amphitheater facing the river. Until the 1960s, when
        they were drowned out by the noise of jets using
        National Airport, open air concerts were performed on
        a floating stage moored in front of the steps. A
        favorite date for a young man in those days was to rent
        a canoe and paddle his girl to one of these concerts.
        A favorite concert was the annual performance of the
        1812 Overture, accompanied by U.S. Army saluting
        cannons lining the riverbank.*

7.2   In one block, at the intersection of New Hampshire
      Avenue and F Street, cross F and walk straight up a
      short hill to the white marble Kennedy Center. (See
      Map 3-2.)

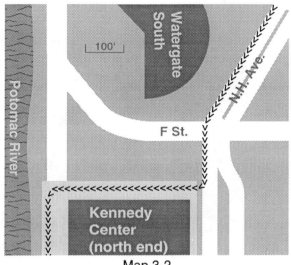

Map 3-2

7.2-   On reaching the nearest (northeast) corner of the
       Kennedy Center building, turn right onto a wide
       pedestrian concourse. (See Map 3-2.) Follow this
       concourse around three sides (north, west, and south)
       of the building to the southeast corner.

       There are public rest rooms and drinking fountains in
       the Kennedy Center.

       The John F. Kennedy Center for the Performing Arts
       opened in 1971 and has become a major cultural
       attraction of the Washington area. The center includes
       a concert hall, an opera house, two theaters, and a film
       institute. The building is located on the site of one of
       Foggy Bottom's principal and longest-lasting
       industries -- the Christian Heurich Brewery. The
       ornate redbrick, copper-roofed brewery was a
       Washington landmark that some consider to have been
       architecturally more interesting than the sterile and
       somewhat grandiose Kennedy Center. The brewery
       closed in 1956, but before the building was demolished
       in 1966, it was home to Washington's renowned Arena
       Stage.

6.8   On reaching the southeast corner of the Kennedy
        Center, leave the pedestrian concourse and walk
        straight (east) across a divided roadway. (See Map
        3-3.) (CAUTION: The last time I was here, there
        was no crosswalk.)

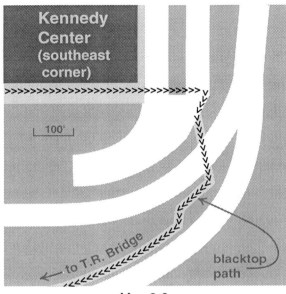

Map 3-3

6.8-   On the other side of the divided roadway, turn right
        onto a sidewalk and then, in a few steps, turn half
        left onto a blacktop path. In a few more steps, walk
        straight across the highway exit ramp and follow the
        blacktop path on the other side. (CAUTION: The
        last time I was here, there was no crosswalk, and you
        may encounter fast-moving traffic entering the exit
        ramp from your left and rear.) In a short distance,
        follow the path onto Theodore Roosevelt Memorial
        Bridge (I-66) crossing the Potomac from D.C. to
        Virginia. (See Map 3-3.)

        Before reaching the Virginia shore, the bridge passes
        over the southern end of Theodore Roosevelt Island, a
        wilderness memorial to the conservationist president.
        If you are lucky, you may see, from your perch on the
        bridge, some of the many large birds that inhabit the
        island, including: great blue herons, black capped

night herons, Canada geese, a variety of ducks, and even an occasional osprey.

6.2   After the walkway follows an exit ramp to the right away from the bridge, and a few steps after the path leads onto a boardwalk, make a U-turn to the right onto another boardwalk. The river should now be to your left.

(NOTE: For the next 1.8 miles the hike closely follows the bank of the river. The highway to your right along this stretch of the hike is the George Washington Memorial Parkway.)

6.0   After passing under the highway ramps leading to and from the Roosevelt Bridge, the boardwalk changes to a blacktop path.

Looking across the river, after passing the southern tip of Roosevelt Island, you come to a position giving an unusual view of the Washington Monument centered directly behind the Lincoln Memorial.

5.5   Follow the path under the western end of the Arlington Memorial Bridge.

5.4   At the intersection with another blacktop path to the right, continue straight along the riverbank.

If you face the river here, the principal landmarks, starting at your extreme left (up-river) and moving to your right, are: the National Cathedral (on the hilltop), the Kennedy Center, the Lincoln Memorial (at the opposite end of Memorial Bridge), the gray stone Romanesque tower of the Old Post Office Building, the redbrick Victorian tower of the original Smithsonian Building, the Capitol, and the white dome of the Jefferson Memorial. This monumental view of the city, plus the grass and shade trees along the river bank, make this an excellent place to rest and have a picnic.

4.7   Continue straight along the riverbank past a small parking area on the right that connects to the George Washington Parkway. Among the trees across the parkway from this parking area, at the Columbia Island Motor Boat Marina, are rest rooms, drinking water, and a small fast-food restaurant with pleasant outdoor seating. (CAUTION: The parkway is a busy, very-fast-moving highway, and while there is a crosswalk a few steps to the right, parkway motorists don't appear to pay much attention to pedestrians.)

4.6   You come to the Navy and Marine Memorial, a graceful sculpture of gulls flying over a cresting wave. Continue along the riverbank, and follow the path around behind the memorial, leaving the memorial to your right.

4.5   Where the path comes to the edge of the parkway, turn left and cross a short bridge spanning a tributary of the Potomac.

4.4   A short distance past the bridge, where the path intersects another blacktop path to the right, turn right onto that path and follow it along a highway exit ramp onto the George Mason Memorial Bridge, crossing the Potomac from Virginia back to D.C.

The George Mason Memorial Bridge is named in honor of the Virginia statesman, patriot, and founding father. The parallel span to your right is named for Jean de Rochambeau, commander of the French forces at the Battle of Yorktown. The two spans together are universally called the 14th Street Bridge because they connect with 14th Street in D.C. This is the approximate location of one of the oldest and most important bridges crossing the Potomac -- the Long Bridge. Built in 1834, the Long Bridge during the Civil War carried the Union Army to and from both victories and disasters in Virginia.

3.8   At the far end of the bridge, where the guard railing on your left ends, make a U-turn to the left down a narrow set of steps. (See Map 3-4.) (NOTE: You have reentered the District of Columbia in the Southwest quadrant of the city. All street signs from here to the end of the hike will include "SW.")

3.8-   After walking straight a short distance from the bottom of the steps, where the walkway comes to a two-lane road, turn right onto a path. (See Map 3-4.)

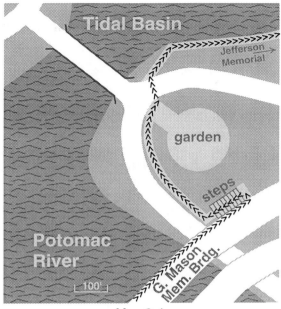

Map 3-4

3.7   Where the path ends, immediately after passing the
       entrance to a small circular garden to your right, turn
       left and cross the road. On the other side of the road,
       turn right onto a path that leads gradually down,
       through the famous Japanese cherry trees, to the
       Tidal Basin. (See Map 3-4.)

3.6   When you reach the bank of the Tidal Basin,
       continue straight onto the concrete path that follows
       the water's edge. As you walk along the edge of the
       basin, the water should be on your left.
       (See Map 3-4.)

       *The Tidal Basin is an artificial body of water created
       from the Potomac by land fill and excavation at the
       end of the 19th century. While the basin now has a
       majestic and monumental character, it was once noted
       more for recreation and entertainment. During the
       late 1910s and early 20s, a popular beach with
       swimming, boating, and dancing was located where
       the Jefferson Memorial now stands.*

3.5   Come to the Jefferson Memorial. There are rest
       rooms and a drinking fountain in the base of the

building. To resume the hike after visiting the memorial, continue in the same direction as before on the path along the edge of the Tidal Basin.

The Jefferson Memorial honors the author of the Declaration of Independence and third president of the U.S. Architecture was one of Jefferson's many avocations, and the dome and columns of the monument are reminiscent of Monticello -- the home Jefferson designed and built for himself near Charlottesville, Virginia. Several quotes of the eloquent president are inscribed within the monument, among them (around the inside base of the dome) the stirring and most characteristic: "I have sworn upon the altar of God eternal hostility against every form of tyranny over the mind of man."

3.4 Continue on the path as it leaves the edge of the Tidal Basin and leads onto a bridge spanning the gates connecting the basin and the Washington Channel of the Potomac. (See Map 3-5.)

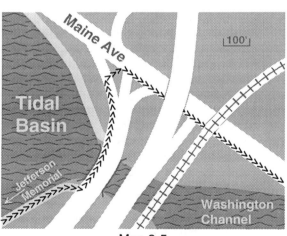

Map 3-5

The Tidal basin was designed with a practical function in mind. Water in the basin, normally maintained at the level of high tide, could be released through the gates at low tide to help maintain the navigability of the Washington Channel. The channel, which you will walk along later in the hike, was home to a busy commercial waterfront from the founding of the city through the early 20th century.

3.3   Just across the bridge, where the path around the
       edge of the Tidal Basin turns off to the left, continue
       straight on the sidewalk that follows the road. (See
       Map 3-5.)

3.3-   In a short distance, at a crosswalk, turn half right and
       cross the roadway to a traffic island. (See Map 3-5.)

3.3-   On the other side of this traffic island, turn half right
       again and follow the large road (Maine Avenue)
       across another traffic island and then under a
       highway bridge. (See Map 3-5.) (CAUTION: The
       last time I passed this way, there were no
       crosswalks.)

3.2   After passing under the highway bridge, continue
       down the right side of Maine Avenue under a
       railroad bridge. (See Map 3-5.)

2.9   After passing a marina on your right and then several
       highway ramps overhead, you come to Washington's
       open-air floating seafood market on your right. (See
       Map 3-6.) The market has decrepit but usable public
       rest rooms, the last available until the end of the
       hike.

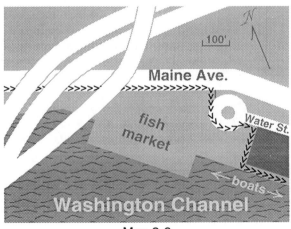

Map 3-6

*Washington's small thriving outdoor seafood market is
located around a set of public wharves. The privately
owned market barges never move. The seafood is
trucked in, much of it from the nearby Chesapeake*

> *Bay. Until fairly recently, however, the wharves were lined with traditional, working "buy boats" that bought seafood directly from Chesapeake watermen and brought it to the city.*

2.9-   Immediately after passing the seafood market and just before coming to a small traffic circle on your right, turn right and follow the sidewalk to the traffic circle. (See Map 3-6.) The circle is at the beginning of Water Street, a road that parallels Maine Avenue.

2.9-   Walk counterclockwise half way around the small traffic circle and then turn right and follow Water Street away from the circle. (See Map 3-6.)

2.8   In a short distance, just before reaching the first of several connected buildings on your right, turn right and walk to the water's edge through the small parking area that is immediately adjacent to the nearest building. The building presently houses a restaurant and the Capitol Yacht Club. (See Map 3-6.)

2.8-   At the water's edge, turn left and walk down the long promenade along the waterfront, past pleasure boats of every type tied up at piers to your right. (See Map 3-6.) Several restaurants line the promenade on your left. Farther on, to your right, is a floating restaurant. At the end of the pier behind the floating restaurant is a lounge in a tower, surrounded, in summer, with outdoor tables.

> *The promenade and restaurants, which replaced a more dilapidated but historic and diverse waterfront, were built as part of the nation's first urban renewal project -- then still called "slum clearance." Beginning in the 1950s, the renewal project covered most of D.C.'s small Southwest quadrant, replacing tightly knit but rundown, largely African American neighborhoods with what planners and architects of the time conceived to be an ideal urban landscape. Today, as a result of the renewal, much of Southwest is architecturally uniform (some say sterile) and largely middle-class with some isolated low income housing.*

2.3   Continue straight on the waterfront promenade past the tourist boat piers and the police and fire boat pier.

2.1   Where the waterfront promenade ends at the Titanic Memorial (the statue of a figure with outstretched arms), turn left (east) onto a wide walkway that follows the old redbrick wall of Fort McNair to your right. This walkway is an extension of P Street.

P Street once led down to the P Street wharf. It was here, in July 1864, during the Civil War, that Union troops brought hurriedly by boat from battlefronts in Virginia, were urgently disembarked to reinforce Fort Stevens in the north of the city. Confederate troops were advancing on Washington and making what turned out to be their only serious threat to the capital.

2.0   At the corner of 4th and P Streets, continue straight (east) on P.

2.0-   In a short distance, at the gate to Fort McNair, turn right (south) into the fort. If you are stopped, tell the sentry that you would like to walk around the fort. Normally visitors are welcome. However, on special occasions -- some presidents have used Fort McNair for jogging -- you may not get in. In such case, skip down to direction at 0.4 below. To continue the hike within Fort McNair, walk straight ahead (south) through the gate onto 3rd Avenue.

Fort McNair, which occupies a narrow, ninety-nine acre site, is named for Lieutenant General Lesley J. McNair who served here as Commanding General of army ground forces from 1942 to 1944, and was later killed in Normandy. The southern part of the site was first used for a defensive battery and later for an arsenal. Beginning in 1826, the Federal Penitentiary of the District of Columbia occupied the northern part. Today the arsenal and penitentiary are gone; the fort acts as headquarters for the U.S. Army Military District of Washington and is home to the National Defense University (formerly the National War College). The university teaches defense policy and strategy to military officers and civilian officials.

1.9   Where 3rd Avenue ends, at its intersection with B
        Street, turn right (west) onto B.

1.9-   In one block, at the intersection of B Street and
        Second Avenue, turn left (south) onto 2nd. There
        should now be a line of quarters for high-ranking
        officers on your right and a parade field to your left.

        *At the far (southern) end of the parade field are
        several tennis courts. Just before the tennis courts
        stands an old brick building, all that remains of the
        Federal Penitentiary. The penitentiary was the site of
        the imprisonment, trial, and hanging of the Lincoln
        assassination conspirators. After their execution, the
        conspirators were buried at an unmarked and
        unknown location within the grounds of the
        penitentiary. Said to haunt the buildings and grounds
        of the fort is the ghost of the lone woman among the
        hanged, Mary Surratt, whose only crime might have
        been that she ran the boarding house where the
        conspirators met.*

1.5   After passing the tennis courts, continue straight on
        2nd Avenue. The green space on either side of 2nd
        Avenue is now a golf course.

1.4   Pass the ornate domed redbrick National War
        College building to your left. (See Map 3-7.)

1.3   Where 2nd Avenue ends, continue in the same
        direction (south) across the grass of the golf course
        to the seawall at the water's edge. (See Map 3-7.)
        The view and the well-placed benches along the sea-
        wall make this an excellent place to stop and rest.

        *The point of land where you stand, at the southern end
        of Fort McNair, is known as Greenleaf Point. Facing
        the water, you are looking south down the Potomac
        River. In the distance, just beyond the high-rise
        buildings on the Virginia (right) bank of the river, is
        the old town of Alexandria. The peninsula to your
        right, which ends just south of where you are standing,
        is Haines Point; beyond it is the main channel of the
        Potomac. The narrow waterway between Fort McNair
        and Haines Point is the Washington Channel, which
        leads back north to D.C.'s waterfront. The large
        tributary to your left is the Anacostia River, leading to*

*the Washington Navy Yard. Haines Point is reclaimed
land; before it was built up, Greenleaf Point was the
southern-most tip of land in the old city and provided
the perfect location for guarding the city against
seaborne invasion from the south. However, the site
played no role in the defense of Washington when the
city was overrun and burned by the British during the
War of 1812. The Redcoats approached by the
Patuxent River (a smaller river roughly paralleling the
Potomac) and attacked the city from the east.
Ironically, however, the site did play an unintentional
role in the debacle. The British accidentally set off
munitions stored in the Greenleaf Point arsenal, killing
thirty of their own soldiers. The arsenal seems to have
been accident prone. During the Civil War, another
disastrous explosion there killed twenty-one women
employed in making rifle cartridges.*

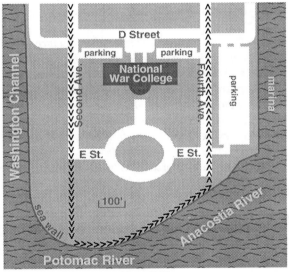

Map 3-7

1.2   To resume the hike, turn left and follow the seawall
       to the east. As you walk along the seawall, the water
       should be to your right. (See Map 3-7.)

       *The small marina ahead of you at the end of the sea-
       wall is where the old Washington City Canal ended.
       The other end of the canal was on the Potomac just
       south of the White House. From there a canal boat
       could travel east, along the present alignment of*

Constitution Avenue, then south, just to the west of the Capitol, to this point on the Anacostia River. The canal was conceived as artery for commerce connecting the parts of the city through which it passed. Instead, it soon became an unused, fetid, sewage-filled barrier isolating most of Southwest Washington from the rest of the city. The canal was filled in and replaced by the existing streets in the late 19th century.

1.1   A short distance before the sea-wall ends, turn left (north) and walk a short distance across the grass and then follow the road to the north. This is 4th Avenue. As you walk north on 4th, you should pass the National War College building to your left. (See Map 3-7.)

0.5   Where 4th Avenue ends at its intersection with B Street, turn left (west) onto B.

The building on your right after you turn onto B Street houses the Commander-in-Chief's Guard -- Company A, 3rd U.S. Infantry. This is part of the ceremonial guard that performs burial details at Arlington National Cemetery. Its soldiers also march at official ceremonies wearing Revolutionary War uniforms and carrying 18th-century flintlocks.

0.5-   At the first intersection, where B Street intersects 3rd Avenue, turn right (north) onto 3rd Avenue.

0.4   After leaving the fort through the gate, make an immediate left turn onto P Street. (When I last visited the fort, there was no street sign for P Street at this intersection.)

0.4-   In a short distance, at the intersection of P and 4th Streets, turn right onto 4th Street.

The four row houses at 1315 to 1321 4th Street were built in 1794 and are known collectively as Wheat Row. They are the oldest group of row houses in the city, and are among the few structures in Southwest that predate the urban renewal of the 1950s and 60s.

0.0   Where 4th Street ends at its intersection with M Street, cross M and continue straight to the

Waterfront Metro station and the end of the hike.
There are public rest rooms and a few restaurants in
the Waterside Mall just beyond the entrance to the
Metro station. Or, if you prefer more atmosphere
and variety, you can walk to the left (west) two
blocks on M Street to reach the waterfront
restaurants you passed earlier in the hike.

NOTES

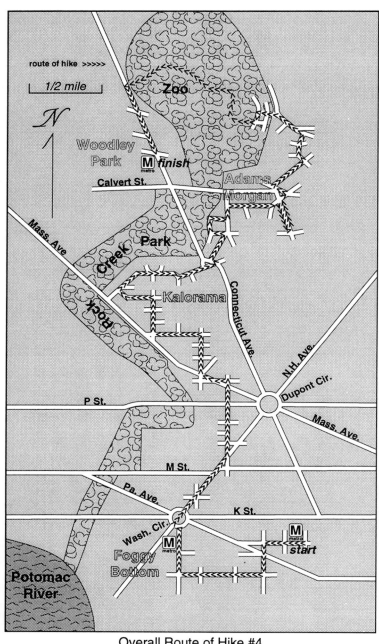

route of hike >>>>>

1/2 mile

N

Zoo

Woodley
Park

M *finish*
metro

Calvert St.

Adams
Morgan

Mass. Ave.

Creek **Park**

Rock

Kalorama

Connecticut Ave.

N.H. Ave.

Dupont Cir.

P St.

Mass. Ave.

M St.

Pa. Ave.

K St.

Wash. Cir.

M *start*
metro

M
metro

Foggy
Bottom

**Potomac
River**

Overall Route of Hike #4
Farragut West to Woodley Park

HIKE #4

Downtown offices and a downtown university; the hospital that saved Ronald Reagan; some grand old mansions; a lovely flight of steps; in-town elegance; the Hispanic downtown and the street of a thousand cafés; descent into the park and an ascent among the animals; and a stroll down the avenue.

From: Farragut West Metro Station (D.C.)

To: Woodley Park Metro Station (D.C.)

Via: I Street, George Washington University, Washington Circle, New Hampshire Avenue, the Spanish Steps, the Kalorama neighborhood, the Adams Morgan neighborhood, the National Zoo, and the Woodley Park neighborhood.

Distance: 5.6 miles

Duration: 3 hours and 45 minutes, if you walk at 2.5 miles per hour, make three 10-minute stops, and take an hour for lunch.

Highlights

The hike begins downtown amid high-rise office buildings. It takes you west through the mid-city campus of the George Washington University. Next, you will hike north past the aging elegance of the Dupont Circle area and then up the lovely, secluded Spanish Steps into the more modern elegance of Kalorama. From Kalorama, you will hike east past the row houses of Adams Morgan and then suddenly burst out upon the busy, cosmopolitan intersection of 18th Street and Columbia Road -- the center of a major Hispanic community. Take a stroll (the sidewalks here are usually too crowded to let you move faster) along both sides of 18th Street, passing a fabulous string of ethnic restaurants. Leaving the busy streets as abruptly as you entered, you will walk past shaded row houses and, eventually, steeply downhill into the cool valley of Rock Creek. From the valley bottom you will take a long uphill trek among the animals in the National Zoological Park. When you leave the zoo you will walk down busy Connecticut

Avenue, through Woodley Park, to the end of the hike at the Woodley Park Metro station.

Things to Know Before You Start

All distances shown in parentheses below indicate miles to the end of the hike.

Intermediate Metro Stations

Foggy Bottom station (4.8 miles).

Places to Stop for a Rest

Convenient places to stop are: George Washington Circle (4.7 miles), the Spanish Steps (3.6 miles), and the Zoo (1.1 to 0.3 miles).

Places to Stop and Eat

This hike passes through one of the most exciting and interesting restaurant districts in the city -- the two blocks of 18th Street between Columbia Road and Kalorama Road (1.9 to 1.7 miles) -- and you may want to schedule your hike so that you arrive there at lunch time. Other places offering a variety of restaurants are P Street in the first block either side of 21st Street (4.0 miles) and Connecticut Avenue in the block south of the Woodley Park Metro station at the end of the hike (0.0 miles).

Public Rest Rooms

The shopping mall at 2000 Pennsylvania Avenue (5.2 miles) and the Zoo (1.1 to 0.3 miles).

On-Route Directions After You Start

Numbers in the left margin indicate miles to the end of the hike. Unless otherwise indicated, maps are oriented north to top of page.

5.6   The Farragut West Metro Station has two exits. Follow the signs to the 18th Street exit. When you reach street level on the escalator, make a U-turn to the right. In a few steps, at the intersection of 18th and I Streets, turn right (west) onto I.

The first part of this hike passes through a corner of Washington's commercial office district, where lawyers, lobbyists, and businessmen meet and work. Not coincidentally, it is also the location of some of the city's more expensive shops and restaurants.

5.4   In two blocks, at the intersection of I and 20th Streets, turn left (south) onto 20th.

Just before crossing Pennsylvania Avenue on 20th Street, in front of you and to your right, is a block of what appear to be restored 19th-century row houses. These are, in fact, merely the facades of those houses, fronting and serving as an integral part of the large, modern building behind them. The controversial design is the result of a compromise between historical preservation and commercial development. The integrated structure is known as 2000 Pennsylvania Avenue, although it actually faces I Street.

5.2   In two short blocks, at the intersection of 20th and H Streets, turn right (west) and walk down the right (north) side of H.

5.2-   In half a block, there is a wide brick walkway leading to the right (north) between two redbrick buildings, into the back of 2000 Pennsylvania Avenue (see description above). A small shopping mall with restaurants, drinking fountains, and rest rooms occupies the ground floor of the complex. These are the last public rest rooms you will pass until near the end of the hike. If you visit the mall, leave the same way you entered and continue the hike by walking west (as before) on H Street.

As you walk along H Street, you are passing through the main campus of George Washington University. The origins of the university can be traced to provisions made in Washington's will, though the institution was not established until 1821. The original school, known as Columbian College, was located in another part of the city. It took its present name in 1909 and moved to its present location in 1912. After the federal government, the university is the largest land owner in the city. It is also one of the city's major land developers.

4.9   At the intersection of H and 23rd Streets, turn right
       (north) onto 23rd.

       *Just after you cross I Street, on your right, is George
       Washington University Hospital. Normally a typical
       busy inner-city hospital, it became the scene of a
       major, nationally televised drama on March 30, 1981.
       That day, President Ronald Reagan was rushed to the
       emergency room after being shot about a mile to the
       north in front of the Washington Hilton Hotel. The
       president underwent several hours of emergency
       surgery and eventually recovered fully. His press
       secretary, Jim Brady, who was shot in the head during
       the assassination attempt and who had initially been
       reported dead, was also treated here. Brady's life was
       saved by the brilliant work of the hospital's surgeons
       but he was left with permanent brain damage. The
       emergency room has since become the Ronald Reagan
       Institute for Emergency Medicine.*

4.7   Where 23rd Street intersects Washington Circle, turn
       left and walk clockwise around the circle. (See Map
       4-1.)

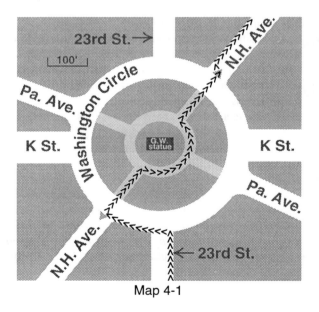

Map 4-1

4.7-   In a short distance, where New Hampshire Avenue
       intersects Washington Circle, cross to the small
       traffic island in the middle of New Hampshire
       Avenue. From there, turn right and cross to the

inside of the circle on the traffic-light-controlled crosswalk. (See Map 4-1.)

4.7-   After crossing to the inside of the circle, walk straight ahead, past the statue of George Washington, to the exact opposite side of the circle. (See Map 4-1.)

4.6   At the opposite side of the circle, at the traffic-light-controlled crosswalk, cross to the small traffic island on the outside of the circle and in the middle of New Hampshire Avenue. From the small traffic island, turn left, cross half of New Hampshire and, on the other side, turn right (northeast) and walk up the left side of the avenue. (See Map 4-1.)

4.3   At the intersection of New Hampshire Avenue and 21st Street, turn half left (north) onto 21st.

After walking several blocks, on your right just before crossing Massachusetts Avenue, is the magnificent Walsh-McLean House, now the Indonesian Embassy. Completed in 1903, the sixty-room mansion was part of the once-grand residential neighborhood that surrounded Dupont Circle (a block to the east). The house was built by Thomas Walsh, who had acquired a fortune from gold mines in the West. Rumor has it that a nugget of gold from one of his mines is hidden somewhere within the structure. Upon Walsh's death, the mansion passed to his daughter Evalyn, wife of the newspaper magnate Edward Beale McLean. Mrs. McLean was the last private owner of the notorious Hope Diamond. Multiple tragedies later afflicted her family and became part of the story of the diamond's alleged curse.

3.9   A few steps after crossing Massachusetts Avenue, at the intersection of 21st and Q Streets, cross and turn left (west) onto Q Street.

The redbrick building on the northwest corner of 21st and Q Streets was built in 1897 as the home of Duncan Phillips, a prodigious collector of contemporary art. Phillips' world-famous art collection is on display in the building.

> *Just past (to the west of) the Phillips mansion is the Embassy of India.*

3.9-   At the next intersection, where Q Street crosses Massachusetts Avenue diagonally, turn half right onto Massachusetts.

> *On your right, just after you turn onto Massachusetts Avenue, is the prestigious Cosmos Club. Built in 1901 as a private residence by railroad tycoon Peter Townshend, the grand design is more evidence of the opulence of the neighborhood at the turn of the century. Oddly, because of a peculiar superstition of Mrs. Townshend's, the mansion was built around the foundation of an older house. The Cosmos Club -- since its inception a haven for men only -- recently gained notoriety for its stubborn, but ultimately unsuccessful, effort to continue to exclude women.*

3.8   At the next intersection, where both Florida Avenue and 22nd Street intersect Massachusetts Avenue, continue straight across Florida and 22nd and then turn right (north) onto 22nd.

> *On crossing Florida Avenue you have entered the exclusive residential neighborhood called Kalorama. The name, meaning "beautiful view" in Greek, was taken from an 18th-century estate whose manor house perched at the top of a rise (in front of you) with a vista overlooking the Potomac. The estate remained essentially rural until the early 20th century -- its inevitable development having been delayed by confusion over how to extend L'Enfant's plan for the city past Florida Avenue. When the area was finally opened up, it attracted many wealthy families, who built mansions in the contemporary revival styles. The neighborhood has been home to four future and former presidents -- Franklin Roosevelt, Herbert Hoover, Woodrow Wilson, and William Howard Taft -- and remains today one of the most elegant and fashionable areas in the city.*

3.6   After crossing Decatur Place, where 22nd Street comes to an end at a set of steps and a small fountain, ascend the steps past the fountain.

*The lovely, secluded, almost secret steps and fountain
are known in the neighborhood as the Spanish Steps.
They were built in 1911-12 by the city's Office of
Public Buildings and Grounds. Imagine what a city
agency would have done with the site today.*

3.6-   A few steps past the top of the Spanish Steps, at the
        first intersection, turn left (west) onto S Street.

*On the left (south) side of S Street, at number 2300,
stands Gales-Hoover House. Now the Embassy of
Myanmar (Burma), the house was built in 1901-02 by
Major Thomas Gales. In 1921 it became the home of
Herbert Hoover while he was Secretary of Commerce
during the Harding administration. The original
manor house of the Kalorama estate stood on this site
until it was demolished in 1888.*

*At number 2320 is the Textile Museum, containing an
eclectic collection of 14,500 textile samples and 1,500
Oriental carpets. The museum is open from 10:00 am
to 5:00 pm Monday through Saturday and 1:00 to 5:00
pm on Sunday.*

*Farther along S Street, at number 2340, is Woodrow
Wilson House. Wilson, after leaving office, moved
here in 1921 with his second wife Edith. In poor
health, he died here in 1924. Edith Wilson continued
to live in the house until her death in 1961. The house
is open to the public Tuesday through Sunday, 10:00
am to 4:00 pm.*

3.4   At the intersection of S and 24th Streets, turn right
        (north) onto 24th.

*On the northeast corner of 24th and S Streets is the
Embassy of Malaysia, with its crescent, star, and
stripes flag.*

3.3   At the intersection of 24th Street and Wyoming
        Avenue, turn left (west) onto Wyoming.

3.1   In one long block, where Wyoming Avenue ends at
        its intersection with Kalorama Road, turn sharply to
        the right onto Kalorama Road.

> *The large detached, Georgian house at 2401 Kalorama Road is known as "The Lindens." Built in 1754, it is, technically, the oldest house in the city. The technicality is that the house was actually built in Danvers, Massachusetts, and was not moved to its present site until 1936. In Massachusetts the house had once served as the summer residence of the last royal governor, Thomas Gage. In Washington it was home to one George Morris, his wife, and their antiques. The Morrises saved the house from demolition in Massachusetts and then had it disassembled, moved, and reassembled where it stands today.*

2.9   At the intersection of Kalorama Road and Kalorama Circle, continue straight on Kalorama Road.

2.8   Where Kalorama Road turns gradually to the right (south) onto 23rd Street, turn left, across 23rd and continue east on Kalorama Road.

> *The large and appropriately chateau-like house on the left side of Kalorama just past 23rd is the residence of the French ambassador. Built in 1911 as the home of a mining magnate, it is the largest house in Kalorama. Just past the French Embassy residence is the Embassy of Portugal and, past that, the Embassy of the Peoples Republic of China, in an appropriately plain tanbrick apartment building. On the right, across from the Portuguese Embassy, is the Embassy of Ethiopia.*

2.6   At the intersection of Kalorama Road and Connecticut Avenue, cross and then turn left onto Connecticut.

2.6-   In a few steps, at the intersection of Connecticut Avenue and Ashmead Place, turn right onto Ashmead.

2.5   In one block, at the intersection of Ashmead Place and Belmont Road, turn sharply to the left onto Belmont. (See Map 4-2.)

2.4   In one block, where Belmont Road turns to the left and Waterside Drive begins on the right, turn right onto Waterside as it follows the edge of Rock Creek Park to your left. (See Map 4-2.)

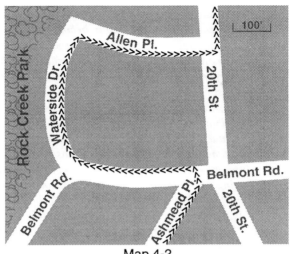

Map 4-2

2.4-   Where Waterside Drive ends at its intersection with
        Allen Place, turn right onto Allen.

2.3   In one block, where Allen Place ends at its
        intersection with 20th Street, cross and then turn left
        onto 20th.

2.2   In one block, at the intersection of 20th and Biltmore
        Streets, turn right onto Biltmore.

2.0   Where Biltmore Street ends at its intersection with
        Columbia Road, cross and then turn left on
        Columbia. (See Map 4-3.)

        *When you arrive at the bustling intersection of
        Columbia Road and 18th Street (a short distance
        ahead) you are at the center of the cosmopolitan
        neighborhood called Adams Morgan. Most of the
        surrounding apartment buildings and row houses were
        built in the early 20th century as residences for upper-
        income families. The commercial parts of the
        neighborhood were much more sedate then, providing
        residents and visitors alike with fashionable shops and
        restaurants. While the early residents were almost
        exclusively native whites, the seeds of diversity were
        also here in the form of professionals from nearby
        Latin American embassies. As in many other city
        neighborhoods, the pressures of the Great Depression
        and World War II, followed by the middle-class flight*

to the suburbs, led to some deterioration. Houses and apartments were subdivided to accommodate a larger and less affluent population, including African Americans and an increasing number of Hispanic immigrants. In recent years the neighborhood has been subject to two population pressures. Waves of immigrants, many of them lower-income Latin Americans fleeing unrest in their native countries, have continued to settle here in ever greater numbers. At the same time, the neighborhood has attracted a very different kind of immigrant -- young, affluent whites fleeing the uniformity and boredom of the suburbs. Hopefully these pressures will remain balanced and this most diverse of all Washington's neighborhoods will continue to provide a haven for all who wish to settle here.

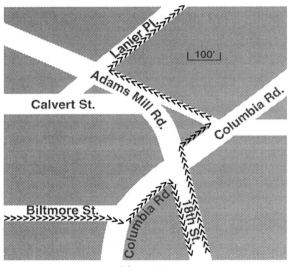

Map 4-3

2.0-   In a few steps, at the major intersection of Columbia Road and 18th Street, turn right (south) and walk down the right (west) side of 18th. (See Map 4-3.)

The next two blocks of 18th Street probably have the densest and most ethnically diverse concentration of restaurants in the metropolitan area. This is the gastronomic equivalent of Embassy Row. If you see a restaurant that interests you on the other side of the street, don't worry; the route of the hike reverses direction and returns along the other side of the street.

1.8   At the intersection of 18th Street and Kalorama
        Road, turn left across 18th and, on the other side,
        turn left again and walk in the opposite direction
        (north) up the east side of 18th.

1.7   At the intersection of 18th Street and Columbia
        Road, continue straight across Columbia Road to a
        traffic island. (See Map 4-3.)

1.7-   On reaching the traffic island, turn right and then
        leave the island by crossing the unnamed access road
        before you. (See Map 4-3.)

1.7-   Across the access road, turn left and follow the road
        straight as it merges into Adams Mill Road. (See
        Map 4-3.)

1.6   In one short block, where Adams Mill Road
        intersects Lanier Place, turn right onto Lanier Place.
        (See Map 4-3.)

        *The small, quaint Engine Company Number 21 on the
        left side of Lanier Place looks as much like a Latin
        American church as a fire house. Built in 1908, it was
        designed to stable the horses that were still used to pull
        fire engines then.*

1.4   In one block, at the intersection of Lanier Place and
        Ontario Road, turn left onto Ontario.

1.4-   In one short block, where Ontario Road turns slightly
        to the left at its intersection with 18th Street, turn
        right onto 18th.

        *The large driveway between Ontario Road and 18th
        Street, at this intersection, leads to the Ontario. Built
        between 1903 and 1906, this is one of the
        neighborhood's early apartment buildings for the
        affluent.*

1.3   In two short downhill blocks, at the intersection of
        18th and Harvard Street, turn left onto Harvard.

1.2   At the bottom of the hill on Harvard Street, at the
        traffic light, bear slightly to the left and cross the

bridge over Rock Creek into the National Zoological
Park. (See Map 4-4.)

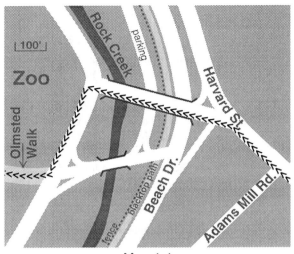

Map 4-4

1.1   On the other side of the bridge, cross the
       intersecting, unmarked road and turn to the left on
       the other side. (See Map 4-4.)

1.1-   In a short distance, turn to the right onto the wide
       walkway leading through the Zoo. (See Map 4-4.)
       This is the Olmsted Walk, which you will follow
       through the Zoo to Connecticut Avenue. Olmsted
       Walk has a number of side trails, so make sure you
       stay on the wide path laid in hexagonal paving tiles.
       Should you become lost, ask for directions to the
       Connecticut Avenue entrance. There are restaurants
       and rest rooms along Olmsted Walk, the first being a
       short distance up the walk on the left. Just a few
       steps up the walk on the right is an information
       booth where you can get a map of the Zoo.

       The National Zoological Park is part of the
       Smithsonian Institution. Founded on this site in 1889,
       the Zoo was designed by Frederick Law Olmsted -- the
       father of American landscape architecture, designer of
       the Capitol grounds and of Central Park in New York.
       The most famous present and past residents of the Zoo
       are Smokey Bear and the giant pandas, Hsing-Hsing
       and Ling-Ling. The panda pair twice gained national
       attention in their attempts to parent offspring.
       Unfortunately, in both attempts the cubs died soon

_after birth, and to add to the misfortune, one of the
parents has also recently died. The Zoo has many
other projects to preserve and breed endangered
species. The Zoo is open daily 8:00 am to 8:00 pm
from April 15 to October 15 and from 8:00 am to 6:00
pm the rest of the year._

0.3   At the Connecticut Avenue entrance to the Zoo,
cross and then turn left onto Connecticut.

_From here to the end of the hike you are walking
through the neighborhood known as Woodley Park.
Around 1800, Philip Barton Key (Frances Scott Key's
uncle) built a manor house nearby and named it
Woodley House. Later developers of the neighborhood
picked up the name presumably because of its
prestigious origins. Along with the rest of Connecticut
Avenue from here north into Maryland, Woodley Park
was first subdivided and developed in the 1890s by a
group of wealthy private investors, who also extended
Connecticut Avenue and opened a new streetcar line.
Although many of the surrounding town houses are
older, most of the apartment buildings along the
avenue were built in the 1920s and 30s._

0.0   On the right side of Connecticut Avenue, just past
Woodley Road, at 24th Street, is the entrance to
Woodley Park Metro station and the end of the hike.
However, you may want to stop at one of the many
nearby restaurants in the next block along both sides
of Connecticut Avenue.

NOTES

_____

_____

_____

_____

_____

_____

_____

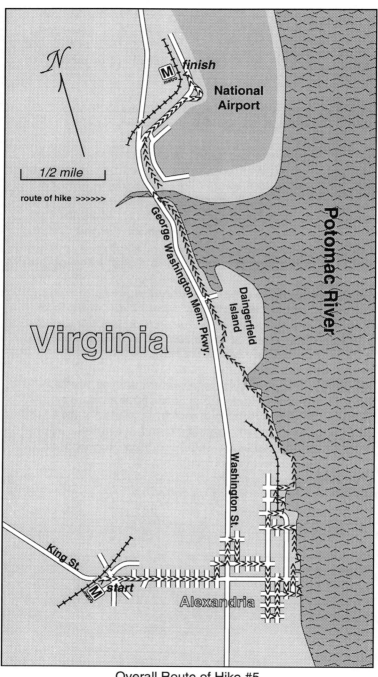

Overall Route of Hike #5
King Street to National Airport

HIKE #5

A walk through a vibrant colonial town among George Washington's haunts, and a trek north along the river bank.

From: King Street Metro Station (Virginia)

To: National Airport Metro Station (Virginia)

Via: Old Town Alexandria (including Christ Church, Gadsby's Tavern, and the Old Presbyterian Meeting House); the Alexandria waterfront and the Torpedo Factory; and the west bank of the Potomac River to National Airport.

Distance: 6.4 miles

Duration: 4 hours if you walk at 2.5 miles per hour and make three 10-minute stops and take an hour for lunch.

Highlights

You will begin this hike at the western edge of Old Town Alexandria and hike east on King Street past small galleries and antique shops. Leaving King Street, you will meander through back streets lined with restored row houses. Some of these streets are still paved in cobblestone. Among the historic sites you will pass are: Christ Church, where George Washington worshiped; Gadsby's Tavern, site of birthday balls held in his honor; and the Old Presbyterian Meeting House, where memorial services were held before the burial of the Father of the Country. Eventually you will reach the Alexandria waterfront, where oceangoing ships still call. The waterfront is also home to the Torpedo Factory, an old World War II munitions plant that has been converted to a center for the creation and display of local arts and crafts. From the waterfront you will hike north along the Virginia bank of the Potomac, through several waterside parks, to the end of the hike at National Airport.

Things to Know Before You Start

All distances given in parentheses below indicate miles to the end of the hike.

Intermediate Metro Stations

None.

Places to Stop for a Rest

Waterfront Park (4.2 miles), Founders Park (3.9 miles), Oronoco Bay Park (3.4 miles), and Tide Lock Park (3.1 miles).

Places to Stop and Eat

Old Town Alexandria offers a superb selection of restaurants, and you may want to schedule your hike accordingly. The route of the hike takes you past restaurants along King Street from the beginning of the hike to Columbus Street (5.8 miles) and, farther on, along King and Union Streets (4.5 to 4.3 miles). If you are interested in authentic colonial atmosphere, try historic Gadsby's Tavern (5.2 miles). In a more modern setting, there is a riverside restaurant directly on the waterfront (4.0 miles) and another at the Daingerfield Island sailing marina (1.7 miles). The hike also offers excellent places to picnic along the river bank at Founders Park (3.9 miles), Oronoco Bay Park (3.4 miles), and Tide Lock Park (3.1 miles). A convenient place to get carry-out is at the "food pavilion" on the waterfront (4.0 miles).

Public Rest Rooms

At the underground parking garage on Fairfax Street (5.0 miles), the Torpedo Factory (4.1 miles), the Daingerfield Island sailing marina (1.7 miles), and National Airport (0.3 miles).

On-Route Directions After You Start

Numbers in the left margin indicate miles to the end of the hike. Unless otherwise indicated, maps are oriented north to top of page.

6.4 The King Street Metro station has only one exit. On leaving the station, turn immediately to the left onto a brick sidewalk that parallels the Metro tracks to your left and an access road to your right. At the first cross street (King Street), turn half right and cross the access road to a long traffic island and then turn half left and cross King Street itself. Across King, turn right (east), away from the Metro tracks and follow King Street east. (See Map 5-1.) In the next several blocks of King Street, you will pass a variety of small restaurants, antique shops, and galleries.

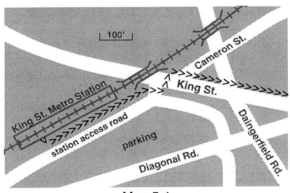

Map 5-1

The first half of this hike threads its way through the historic portion of the pre-Revolutionary city of Alexandria. As you move east toward the Potomac River, you will enter progressively older parts of the city. Named for its founder, the Scottish merchant John Alexander, the site was first settled 1695, though it was not organized as a city until 1749. Alexandria and Georgetown (several miles upriver), were important, thriving seaports well before the formation of the District of Columbia. As a young man, George Washington helped lay out the city's streets and in later life was a frequent visitor from his home at Mount Vernon, nine miles downriver. Though still functioning today as a minor seaport, Alexandria is now known primarily for its large and diverse collection of colonial buildings.

5.8 After a number of blocks, at the intersection of King and Columbus Streets, cross and then turn left

(north) onto Columbus. (If, however, you're looking
for a place to eat, the next block of King past
Columbus has several more restaurants to choose
from. But keep in mind that you will come to many
more restaurants farther along in the hike.)

*On the right side of the Columbus Street, in the first
block, is the historic Christ Church. This was the
church of George Washington, Robert E. Lee, and
many other famous Virginians. Further, it has been a
tradition for Presidents of the U.S. to attend services
here sometime during their term in office. The church
has also had several noteworthy rectors, including
William Meade, who later became Presiding Bishop of
the Episcopal Church of the Confederate States of
America. The Georgian style building was completed
in 1773. It is open to the public Monday through
Saturday from 9:00 am to 4:00 pm and Sunday from
2:00 to 4:30 pm.*

5.7   At the intersection of Columbus and Cameron
        Streets, just past Christ Church, turn right (east) onto
        Cameron.

5.6   In one block, at the intersection of Cameron and
        Washington Streets, turn left (north) onto
        Washington.

        *Take a look at the plaque on Washington Street
        between Cameron and Queen Streets marking the
        former site of the Beth El Hebrew Congregation.*

5.5   In two blocks, at the intersection of Washington and
        Princess Streets, turn right (east) onto Princess.

        *Notice the small marker in the center of Princess Street
        describing the cobblestones used to pave the street.*

5.4   In one block, at the intersection of Princess and St.
        Asaph Streets, turn right (south) onto St. Asaph.

5.2   In two blocks, at the intersection of St. Asaph and
        Cameron Street, cross and then turn left (east) onto
        Cameron.

        *On the southwest corner of Cameron and Royal
        Streets stands historic, exquisitely Georgian Gadsby's*

Tavern. The original part of the tavern, now a museum, was built around 1770. A larger addition went up in 1792 and was known as the City Hotel. Gadsby's Tavern was a popular gathering place for the colonial and early federal elite, and has been the site of patriot meetings, society balls, and receptions for presidents. George and Martha Washington attended an annual ball here held on the General's birthday. It was on the steps of the tavern that Washington performed his last military review. You can still get a meal in the tavern, served by a staff in period dress. The entrance is around the corner on Royal Street.

The brick building on the right side of Cameron extending from Royal to Fairfax Street is the Alexandria City Hall. Though the interior of the building has been renovated into modern offices, the exterior is preserved in its original early 20th-century form.

5.0   Immediately past City Hall, at the intersection of Cameron and Fairfax Streets, turn right (south) onto Fairfax. In the first block of Fairfax, to the right down a ramp to an underground parking lot, are public rest rooms.

In the first block of Fairfax Street on the left is Carlyle House. Built by a Scottish merchant in 1752, it is a fine example of a large in-town colonial dwelling. The house is historically important because it was here that the British General Braddock and several Royal governors proposed the hated Stamp Act, which helped touch off the Revolutionary War.

Several blocks down Fairfax Street, on the right side after crossing Duke Street, you come to the Old Presbyterian Meeting House. The church was built in 1774 to serve the Scottish population of the city. On a cold winter day in 1799 the memorial service for George Washington was held here. The churchyard in the rear contains several old graves, including the Tomb of the Unknown Soldier of the Revolutionary War.

4.7   After passing the Old Presbyterian Meeting House, at the intersection of Fairfax and Wolfe Streets, turn left (east) onto Wolfe.

4.7-   In one block, at the intersection of Wolfe and Lee Streets, turn left (north) onto Lee.

          The Athenaeum, on the northwest corner of Lee and Prince Streets, is one of the city's few surviving examples of Greek revival architecture. It was originally built as bank in 1852 and later became a church. It is now a fine arts exhibit hall.

4.5   In three blocks, at the intersection of Lee and King Streets, turn right (east) onto King. A variety of restaurants front this block of King Street.

4.4   In one block, at the intersection of King and Union Streets, turn right (south) onto Union.

4.3   In one block, at the intersection of Union and Prince Street, turn left (east) onto Prince.

4.3-   In one short block, cross Strand Street and walk in the same direction (east) on a walkway, through Waterfront Park, to the bank of the Potomac River.

4.2   At the river, turn left (north) and follow the path along the water's edge. Where the park ends, follow the path to the left (west) away from the river bank.

4.1   Where the path returns to Strand Street, turn right (north) onto Strand. (CAUTION: There are no sidewalks along Strand Street here.)

4.1-   In a short distance, where Strand ends at its intersection with King Street, cross King and continue in the same direction (north) onto a redbrick walkway between two buildings. (See Map 5-2.)

4.1-   In a short distance the path leads onto a boardwalk along the water's edge. (See Map 5-2.) The concrete building to your left is the Torpedo Factory. Just inside its doors are rest rooms and drinking fountains.

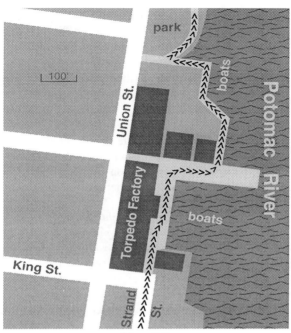

Map 5-2

The Torpedo Factory Fine Arts Center and Archaeological Museum is open to the public and contains the studios of a number of local artists and craftsmen. Although it is difficult to visualize today, this was once an industrial waterfront and the building was indeed originally a factory producing torpedoes for the U.S. Navy. The factory was built in 1918, and continued to manufacture munitions through World War II. On display inside is one of the factory's principal products, the MK-14 torpedo. Following World War II, the building became a federal storehouse containing everything from dinosaur bones to Nazi war records. The city bought the site in 1969, and over the next fourteen years developed it into what you see around you today.

4.0   At the far (north) end of the Torpedo Factory, turn right (east) and continue along the water's edge past a food pavilion and a restaurant on your left. (See Map 5-2.)

4.0-   Just past the restaurant, turn left (north) and follow
       the path along the water's edge. (See Map 5-2.)

3.9   Where the walkway comes to Founders Park and a
       ship's anchor, turn to the right and follow the gravel
       path along the river bank through the park. (See
       Map 5-2.)

3.7   Where the path along the river bank ends at a city
       street, turn left (west) and follow the sidewalk on the
       left side. You are now on Oronoco Street, but the
       last time I passed here, there was no street sign.

       *The platform on the right, where Oronoco Street
       begins at the river bank, provides a place to watch
       ships load and unload. As you might guess, given the
       metropolitan area's primary industry, the principal
       cargo unloaded here seems to be paper.*

3.7-   At the intersection of Oronoco and Union Streets, at
       the western edge of the park, cross Union and
       continue straight (west) on Oronoco.

3.6   At the intersection on Oronoco and Fairfax Streets,
       turn right onto Fairfax.

3.5   In one block, at the intersection of Fairfax and
       Pendleton Streets, cross and then turn right onto
       Pendleton.

3.4   Where railroad tracks diagonally cross Pendleton
       Street, just before the street turns to the right, turn to
       the left, enter Oronoco Bay Park on a gravel path,
       and follow the river bank north.

3.3   Where the path ends at its intersection with Madison
       Street (the street that provides access to the
       Alexandria Schools Rowing Facility) turn left (west)
       and follow Madison away from the river. (See Map
       5-3.) (NOTE: This and the next three directions take
       you around an area, north of the rowing facility, that
       was under development the last time I was here.
       When this development is completed, there will
       probably be a path allowing you to continue north
       past the Rowing Facility, along the river bank.)

3.3-   Immediately after crossing railroad tracks, turn right
        (north) onto a blacktop path that follows the tracks.
        (See Map 5-3.)

3.2   At the first intersection of the blacktop path with a
        road, turn right (east) and follow the road back
        toward the river. The road is Montgomery Street,
        but when I was last here there was no street sign.
        (See Map 5-3.)

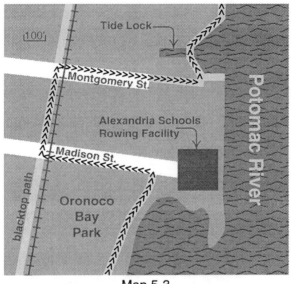

Map 5-3

3.1   Where Montgomery Street ends, continue straight on
        a blacktop path toward the river and into Tide Lock
        Park. (See Map 5-3.)

3.1-   In a few steps, follow the path as it turns to the left to
        a bridge over the tide lock entrance to the historic,
        but now defunct, Alexandria Canal. From here
        continue north, along the river bank, through Tide
        Lock Park. (See Map 5-3.)

        *The Alexandria Canal connected Alexandria with the
        eastern terminus, in Georgetown, of the 187-mile-long
        C&O Canal. Paralleling the west bank of the
        Potomac, the Alexandria Canal allowed canal boats
        that had carried cargoes to Georgetown from points as
        far distant as Cumberland, Maryland, to continue*

south to the larger port at Alexandria -- a few critical miles closer to the ocean in the days of sail.

2.8   At the end of Tide Lock Park, follow a blacktop path that makes switchbacks up a short grade to the left away from the river bank. At the top of the grade, where the path ends at its intersection with another blacktop path, turn right onto the other path. (CAUTION: Most of the rest of the hike follows pathways used by fast-moving bicyclists. It is a good idea to walk well to the right side on the path, and be ready to make way when you hear cyclists approaching from behind.)

2.5   The path passes immediately behind a large power plant.

2.3   The path passes behind a high-rise building on a boardwalk and then turns away from the river bank and into a wooded area.

2.1   At a triangular intersection with another blacktop path, bear to the right onto the other path. From here on, the path roughly parallels the George Washington Memorial Parkway to your left.

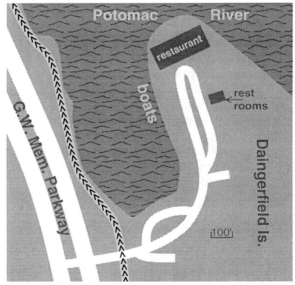

Map 5-4

1.7   Where the path crosses a small road that intersects with the George Washington Parkway, continue straight across the road. Note, however, that if you follow this road to the right, you will come to the Daingerfield Island sailing marina, where you will find rest rooms, water, and a restaurant with a bar and outdoor terraces. (See Map 5-4.) You are now close to the end of the hike, and this makes a good place to stop for a drink and a snack -- or even a full meal.

1.0   The path comes to the edge of the George Washington Parkway and follows the parkway on a bridge over a tributary of the Potomac.

1.0-   Immediately after crossing the bridge, bear to the left through a triangular intersection with another blacktop path. The hike now leaves the river bank and skirts the edge of National Airport to your right. The George Washington Parkway is still to your left. Parallel to the path on your right is an airport access road.

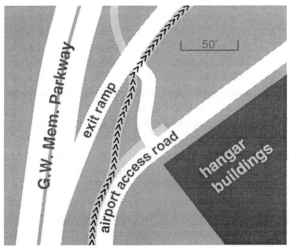

Map 5-5

0.7   As you near a line of large airport hangar buildings to your right, the path follows the left edge of the airport access road. Then, as the access road turns gradually to the right around the corner of the line of hangar buildings, follow the blacktop path as it turns to the left, away from the access road. Do not continue along the edge of the access road onto the concrete sidewalk. (See Map 5-5.)

0.6   In a short distance, where the blacktop path leads onto a crosswalk over an exit ramp of the parkway, turn half right away from the blacktop path, cross a small road, and follow a concrete sidewalk up the right side of the exit ramp. (See Map 5-5.) Follow this sidewalk to the passenger terminal buildings of the airport. There are rest rooms, drinking fountains, snack bars, restaurants, and a cocktail lounge in the passenger terminal.

       (NOTE: At press time the terminal area at National Airport was undergoing major redevelopment, and the following directions will eventually become outdated. If you are at all confused about where to go, ask for directions to the National Airport Metro station.)

0.3   On reaching the semicircular-shaped passenger terminal complex, cross over the traffic lane to your right and continue in the same direction on the sidewalk that leads around directly past the front of the buildings, leaving them to your right and the multi-lane terminal access roads to your left.

       The original National Airport terminal building is under the control tower toward the end of the semicircle. This building was finished in 1940, and its interior includes some wonderful Art Deco reminders of the days when air travel was still romantic.

0.1   After passing the end of the semicircular terminal buildings, follow the signs pointing to the Metro station. (NOTE: When the terminal redevelopment is complete, you will probably need to enter the terminal building and follow the signs inside to the Metro station.)

0.0   Arrive at the National Airport Metro station and the end of the hike.

NOTES

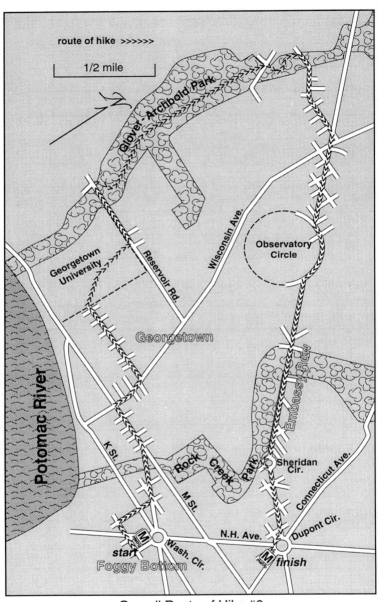

Overall Route of Hike #6
Foggy Bottom to Dupont Circle

HIKE #6

An infamous alley; some of Washington's most popular nightspots; restored grandeur; a visit with the Jesuits; a long walk through the woods; and a trip past foreign outposts.

From: Foggy Bottom Metro Station (D.C.)

To: Dupont Circle Metro Station (D.C.)

Via: The Foggy Bottom neighborhood, M Street and Wisconsin Avenue, west Georgetown, Georgetown University, Glover-Archbold Park, Massachusetts Avenue and Embassy Row, and Dupont Circle.

Distance: 6.4 miles

Duration: 3 hours if you walk at 2.5 miles per hour and make three 10-minute stops.

Highlights

The hike begins in the restored, one-time industrial working-class neighborhood of Foggy Bottom. From there you will follow Pennsylvania Avenue west to M Street and then Wisconsin Avenue -- the principal commercial streets of Georgetown and a major center of Washington nightlife. Leaving Wisconsin Avenue, you will walk west along O Street, past beautifully restored row-house mansions, to the campus of Georgetown University. After walking through the campus, you will go west along Reservoir Road and then north through the hardwood forest valley of Glover-Archbold Park. You will then climb out of the valley on Cathedral Avenue and turn onto Massachusetts Avenue near the National Cathedral and Mt. Saint Albans, one of the highest points in the city. Finally, you will descend along Massachusetts Avenue -- past Embassy Row and some palatial old mansions -- to the Bohemian precinct of Dupont Circle and the end of the hike.

Things to Know Before You Start

All distances shown in parentheses below indicate miles to the end of the hike.

Intermediate Metro Stations

None.

Places to Stop for a Rest

Convenient rest stops along the route are the Georgetown University campus (4.9 miles) and the small park at the intersection of Wisconsin and Massachusetts Avenues (2.3 miles).

Places to Stop and Eat

There are many places to eat along M Street and Wisconsin Avenue (5.8 to 5.3 miles) but this is early in the hike. More convenient are the many restaurants within a block or two of Dupont Circle (0.0), at the end of the hike.

Public Rest Rooms

Only in the Intercultural Center on the Georgetown University campus (4.7 miles).

Some Cautions

More than a mile of this hike follows a dirt trail through the woods of Glover-Archbold Park. This trail can be muddy and slippery when wet.

On-Route Directions After You Start

Numbers in the left margin indicate miles to the end of the hike. Unless otherwise indicated, maps are oriented north to top of page.

6.4   The Foggy Bottom Metro station has only one exit. When you reach street level on the escalator, make a U-turn to the right and walk west through a small linear park that constitutes I Street between 23rd and 24th Streets.

6.4-   Where the park ends at its intersection with 24th
        Street, continue straight (west) onto I.

        This is the neighborhood called Foggy Bottom, known
        today for its quaint, restored row houses and expensive
        high-rise residential buildings. But the affluence of the
        today's Foggy Bottom belies its history. In the 19th
        century Foggy Bottom was an industrial area centered
        on the transportation provided by the nearby Potomac
        River and C&O Canal. The small row houses were
        built for the primarily Irish and German workers in
        these industries. With the decline and closing of the
        canal in the early 20th century, most of the local
        industries relocated to the rail yard district in
        Northeast Washington, and Foggy Bottom became
        economically depressed and run down. Restoration of
        the blighted neighborhood began in the 1950s and
        advanced rapidly as a spontaneous, mostly private
        phenomenon.

6.3   At the intersection of 25th and I Streets, cross and
        then turn right (north) onto 25th.

        On the right side of 25th Street, in the middle of the
        block north of I Street, is the entrance to the infamous
        Snow's Court. More than 300 people were once
        crammed into the tiny quarters of the alley, first Irish
        immigrants and then African Americans. It was
        considered to be one of the most overcrowded, filthy,
        crime infested parts of the city. Today what remains of
        these quarters has been restored into fashionable row
        houses.

6.1   In two blocks, at the intersection of 25th Street and
        Pennsylvania Avenue, turn left (northwest) onto
        Pennsylvania.

5.8   At the intersection of Pennsylvania Avenue and 29th
        Street, follow Pennsylvania as it turns slightly to the
        left (west) and becomes M Street.

        On the right side of M, opposite its intersection with
        Thomas Jefferson Street, stands the Old Stone House.
        The building, which has served a variety of mundane
        functions throughout its history, is the only surviving
        pre-Revolutionary building in the city. For much of

*the 19th century it avoided demolition probably
because it was mistakenly believed to have been Suter's
Tavern -- the site where George Washington convinced
local land owners to sell their property to form the
nation's capital and where Pierre L'Enfant laid out the
plans for the new city.*

*This stretch of M Street, along with Wisconsin Avenue
ahead of you, forms the commercial center of
Georgetown, offering many fine shops and restaurants.
Much against the wishes of the surrounding residents,
the area is also a major center of nightlife, attracting
many tourists and swarms of young people on
weekends. It has often been assumed that Georgetown
has no Metro station because the residents were
opposed to making their neighborhood any more
accessible to this evening onslaught.*

5.5   At the intersection of M Street and Wisconsin
        Avenue, cross and then turn right (north) onto
        Wisconsin.

5.3   In three blocks, at the intersection of Wisconsin
        Avenue and O Street, turn left (west) onto O.

*As you leave busy Wisconsin Avenue on O Street you
enter an exclusive neighborhood of restored, high-
priced town houses typical of Georgetown today. The
houses date from the early to the late 19th century.
Georgetown's reputation as the home of Washington's
social and governmental elite can be traced back to the
founding of the Nation's Capital, when Georgetown --
then a thriving, independent port city -- offered the
best and most established housing in the area. But
Georgetown has also passed through hard times.
Toward the end of the 19th century the economy of the
port began to deteriorate. At about the same time, new
streetcar lines led to new suburban development,
providing an attractive alternative for upper-income
families. By the 1920s the port was mostly defunct and
the residential areas had declined dreadfully. At about
this same time, however, a restoration movement
began. The movement accelerated during the
Roosevelt administration as many of the influential
"New Dealers" moved in, attracted to Georgetown's
small-town southern charm. The restoration
movement climaxed in 1950, when the Old*

Georgetown Act was passed by the Congress, giving the area special historical status. The final act in Georgetown's regained prestige came when Senator John F. Kennedy and his brother Robert, along with their families, took up residence.

4.9   At the intersection of O and 37th Streets, continue straight (west) between the gate houses of the Georgetown University campus. (See Map 6-1.)

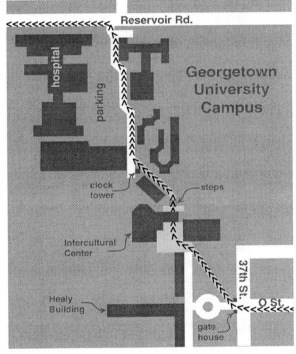

Map 6-1

4.9- Just past the gate houses, before reaching a small traffic circle, turn half right (northwest) onto a brick walkway that crosses a lawn. (See Map 6-1.)

Georgetown University was established in 1789 and is the oldest university in the city and the oldest Catholic University in the United States. The towered building facing the entrance gate dates from the university's earliest days; George Washington once addressed the students from its front steps. This is the Healy Building, named for Rev. Patrick F. Healy, who was *president of the university from 1874 to 1882. Father Healy is probably the person most responsible for expanding Georgetown from a small college to a major educational institution. He was also the first African American president of a major American college.*

4.7   After reaching a small plaza area, turn half right (north) and walk through an opening in the right-hand end of a redbrick building (the Intercultural Center), then up a flight of steps onto a walkway that turns gradually half left (northwest). (See Map 6-1.) There are public rest rooms in the Intercultural Center.

4.6   After passing a clock tower on your left, turn half right (north) onto the sidewalk that follows the right side of a small road. Follow this road generally north through the campus past a parking area to your left. (See Map 6-1.)

4.5   Immediately after exiting the campus, where the campus road intersects Reservoir Road, turn to the left (west) and walk down the left (south) side of Reservoir. (See Map 6-1.)

4.1   After passing the French Embassy on your right, Reservoir Road traverses the wooded Glover-Archbold Park. Near the far side of the park, where Reservoir intersects 44th Street, turn right (north) and cross Reservoir at the crosswalk. On the other side of Reservoir, continue straight (north) into the woods on the dirt Glover-Archbold Trail. (See Map 6-2.)

4.0   Follow the trail downhill and, immediately after crossing a small stream bed, follow the main trail as it turns left. The stream bed should now be to your left. For some distance the trail generally follows the alignment of a large, buried concrete culvert. In some places, where the culvert is exposed, you walk directly atop it. (See Map 6-2.)

Glover-Archbold Park takes in most of a small stream valley extending northward from the Potomac River three miles into the residential areas of Northwest Washington. The stream is called Foundry Branch --

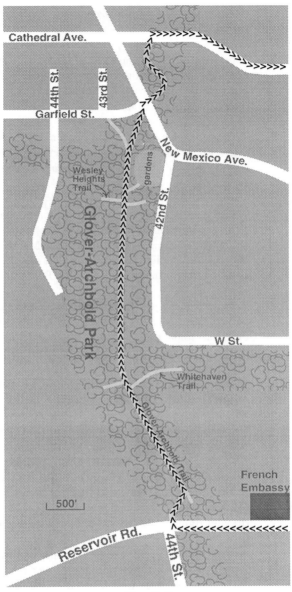

Cathedral Ave.

44th St.

43rd St.

Garfield St.

New Mexico Ave.

Wesley Heights Trail

gardens

42nd St.

Glover-Archbold Park

W St.

Whitehaven Trail

Glover-Archbold Trail

French Embassy

500'

Reservoir Rd.

44th St.

Map 6-2

named for Foxall's Foundry, which was located near
the C&O Canal, about half a mile downstream. The
park is a hardwood forest that includes oak, tulip
poplar, elm, beech, hickory, and sycamore. Many bird
varieties inhabit the park, including the large pileated
woodpecker. Most of the land for the park was

> *donated in 1924 by two prominent Washingtonians, Ann Archbold and Charles C. Glover.*

3.7   Where the dirt Whitehaven Trail leads to the right, continue straight on the Glover-Archbold Trail. The last time I was here, a trail sign marked this intersection. (See Map 6-2.)

3.7-   A short distance past the Whitehaven Trail intersection, continue straight past an unmarked trail leading to your left across the stream bed. (See Map 6-2.)

3.2   A few steps before the trail takes you along the top of an exposed section of the culvert, continue straight past an intersecting trail. (See Map 6-2.) When I was last here, a sign to the left identified the crossing trail as the Wesley Heights Trail.

3.2-   A short distance past the exposed section of the culvert, continue straight past a small, unmarked trail that leads to the right into what is presently a community vegetable garden. (See Map 6-2.)

3.1   Where the trail branches at a Y-shaped intersection, follow the branch to the right. (See Map 6-2.)

3.1-   The trail crosses a wooden bridge over the stream bed.

3.0   Where the trail leaves the woods, at the intersection of New Mexico Avenue and Garfield Street, cross Garfield (to your left) and then cross New Mexico (to your right) at the crosswalk. (When I was last here, there were no street signs.) On the other side of New Mexico, walk straight from the crosswalk into the woods and back onto the Glover-Archbold Trail. From here the trail descends to the bottom of the stream valley. (See Map 6-2.)

2.9   The trail turns gradually to the left, ascends, and then follows the western boundary of the park near some high rise apartment buildings to your left. (See Map 6-2.)

2.8   After ascending a set of wooden steps, where the trail leaves the woods and intersects Cathedral

Avenue (unmarked when I was last here), cross and
then turn right onto Cathedral. (See Map 6-2.)
(CAUTION: No crosswalk exists for Cathedral
Avenue.)

2.3   At the intersection of Cathedral and Massachusetts
Avenues, turn right (southeast) across Cathedral and
walk along the right side of Massachusetts. From
here, you will follow Massachusetts Avenue to
Dupont Circle, where the hike ends.

2.3-   In a short distance, cross Wisconsin Avenue and
continue straight on Massachusetts. (NOTE: Before
crossing Wisconsin, a few steps to the right (south) is
a restaurant and a small food store. Across
Wisconsin is a small park with benches and drinking
water.)

*A short distance north on Wisconsin Avenue, visible
over the treetops, stand the Gothic towers of the
Washington National Cathedral. Farther down
Massachusetts Avenue, on the left side, at its
intersection with 36th Street, is the Saint Sophia Greek
Orthodox Cathedral. Still farther down
Massachusetts, on the right, just before its intersection
with Edmunds Street, stands the Russian Orthodox
Church of Saint Nicholas.*

1.8   At the intersection of Massachusetts Avenue and
Observatory Circle, follow Massachusetts as it turns
slightly to the left and follows the circular perimeter
of the U.S. Naval Observatory grounds on your
right.

*A little farther down Massachusetts, between the two
white anchors, is the entrance to the grounds of the
U.S. Naval Observatory. The Navy uses the
observatory to prepare navigation tables and to
develop and test precise clocks. Just before crossing
the road leading into the observatory grounds, look
through the gate and you will see, on a hilltop, the
large, steep-roofed Admirals House -- formally the
residence of the Chief of Naval Operations and now
the home of the Vice President.*

1.5   At the (second) intersection of Massachusetts
        Avenue and Observatory Circle, continue to follow
        Massachusetts as it turns slightly to the left, away
        from the observatory grounds.

        *A short distance down Massachusetts from
        Observatory Circle, you pass the British Embassy on
        your right and, just past the embassy, a statue of
        Winston Churchill. Directly across Massachusetts
        from the embassy is a small park dedicated to the
        Lebanese poet Kahlil Gibran.*

        *The stretch of Massachusetts Avenue from the British
        Embassy southeast to Dupont Circle is known as
        Embassy Row. As you walk down Embassy Row, you
        will pass the sovereign territories of: Bolivia, South
        Africa, Iran, Brazil, Japan, Bahamas, Venezuela,
        Zambia, Tunisia, Cote d'Ivoire, Malaysia, Malawi,
        Paraguay, Madagascar, Korea, Cameroon, Austria,
        the Sultanate of Oman, Pakistan, Burkina Faso, Haiti,
        Turkey, Romania, Greece, Ireland, Sudan, Croatia,
        Togo, Luxembourg, and Indonesia.*

1.1   Continue on Massachusetts Avenue as it crosses on a
        bridge over the wooded Rock Creek Park.

        *On the left side of Massachusetts Avenue, just past
        Rock Creek Park, is the picturesque, intricately
        decorated Washington Islamic Center. The mosque is
        oriented on the site so that it faces Mecca. Dedicated
        in 1957, the center is designed principally to serve
        Muslim members of Washington's diplomatic corps.*

0.6   At the intersection of Massachusetts Avenue and
        Sheridan Circle, walk half way around the circle to
        the right and continue southeast down
        Massachusetts.

        *The statue in the center of the circle is of General
        Philip Sheridan, the tenacious and successful Union
        cavalry officer. The statue, sculpted by Gutzon
        Borglum (creator of Mount Rushmore), was erected in
        1909, within sight of the home of Sheridan's widow,
        2211 Massachusetts. The circle is also the site of a car
        bombing in 1976 that killed Orlando Letelier, former
        ambassador to the U.S. from the Chilean Marxist
        government of Salvador Allende. Allende was*

overthrown and executed in a right-wing military coup d'état. An American colleague of Letelier's, Ronny Moffitt, was also killed in the car bombing.

The town house on Sheridan Circle at 2306 Massachusetts Avenue is known as Studio House. Built in 1902, it served as the home and studio for Alice Pike Barney, a playwright and painter. A woman of means, she was known as much for entertaining artistic notables of the day as for her own artistic creations.

On crossing 22nd Street, you enter the neighborhood centered on and named for Dupont Circle. (Dupont Circle is a few blocks ahead of you at the end of the hike.) During the late 19th and early 20th centuries this was the city's grandest and most fashionable residential area. While the neighborhood is now home to the somewhat less affluent, there remain a few reminders of past opulence. Just after you cross Q Street, on your right, is Anderson House. Now headquarters of the Society of the Cincinnati, it was built at the turn of the century by Lars Anderson, a wealthy diplomat. Just after crossing 21st Street, on your right, is the fabulous Walsh-McLean House. Now the Indonesian Embassy, this 60-room mansion was built in 1903 by Thomas Walsh, a man who had made a fortune in Western gold mining. Just before crossing 20th Street, on your right, is the dark-brick Victorian Blaine Mansion, built in 1881 by Senator James G. Blaine, a founder of the Republican Party and a three-time presidential candidate.

0.1   Where Massachusetts Avenue intersects Dupont Circle, turn right and follow the circle counterclockwise. (When last here, I found no street sign marking the circle.)

Though Dupont Circle was once the center of a fashionable neighborhood, it has been famous more recently for its role as a gathering place for hippies and leftist political radicals in the 1960s. The circle is much tamer today, although it is still populated much of the time with a slightly Bohemian crowd. The circle was named for the Civil War admiral (Union, of course) Samuel Francis Dupont.

0.0   About one-quarter of the way around Dupont Circle,
       where it intersects 19th Street, is the entrance to the
       Dupont Circle Metro station and the end of the hike.

       Near Dupont Circle are many restaurants. The
       closest concentrations are west of the circle on P
       Street and north of the circle along both sides of
       Connecticut Avenue.

NOTES

_____
_____
_____
_____
_____
_____
_____
_____
_____
_____
_____
_____
_____
_____
_____
_____
_____
_____
_____
_____
_____
_____
_____
_____
_____
_____
_____
_____
_____
_____
_____
_____
_____
_____

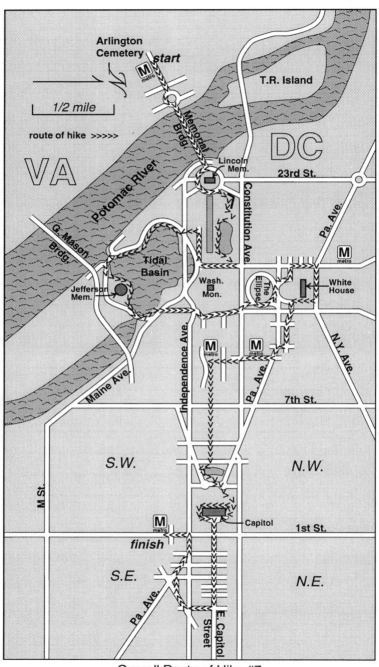

Overall Route of Hike #7
Arlington Cemetery to Capitol South

HIKE #7

The grand tour of the monumental city plus a little walk through a quiet old neighborhood.

From: Arlington Cemetery Metro Station (Virginia)

To: Capitol South Metro Station (D.C.)

Via: Memorial Bridge, the Lincoln Memorial, the Vietnam Veterans Memorial, Constitution Gardens, the Tidal Basin, the Jefferson Memorial, the Bureau of Engraving and Printing, the U.S. Holocaust Museum, the Washington Monument, the Ellipse, the White House, Pennsylvania Avenue, the Old Post Office Building, the museums and galleries of the Mall, the Capitol and its grounds, and Capitol Hill.

Distance: 9.0 miles

Duration: 5 hours 5 minutes if you walk at 2.5 miles per hour, make six 10-minute stops, and take half an hour for lunch.

Highlights

From the Arlington Cemetery Metro station, the hike crosses Memorial Bridge to the Lincoln Memorial and then takes you to the nearby Vietnam Veterans Memorial. You will then walk east past the pond in Constitution Gardens and then south among the cherry trees on the edge of the Tidal Basin, to the Jefferson Memorial. Turning northward next, you will follow Raoul Wallenberg Place past the Bureau of Engraving and Printing and the Holocaust Museum, and then cross the Mall by the Washington Monument to the Ellipse. On the north side of the Ellipse, the hike passes the National Christmas Tree and the south lawn of the White House and then takes you north, past the elegant architectural splendor of the Old Executive Office Building to Pennsylvania Avenue and the north entrance of the White House. You will now turn south, walk between the White House and the Treasury Building, and then east down the grand ceremonial stretch of Pennsylvania Avenue toward the Capitol. Arriving at the

towering, Romanesque Old Post Office Building, you will turn
south and return to the Mall. Then you will hike east down
the center of the Mall -- past museums, art galleries, and the
Smithsonian "Castle" -- to the Capitol grounds, where you will
visit a secret grotto and get a magnificent view of the city
through which you have just hiked. Leaving the Capitol
grounds, you will pass the Supreme Court and the Library of
Congress, then meander among the restored row houses of
Capitol Hill and arrive at the Capitol South Metro station and
the end of the hike.

Things to Know Before You Start

*All distances shown in parentheses below indicate miles to the
end of the hike.*

Intermediate Metro Stations

Three intermediate Metro stations are located along the route
-- Farragut West, one block north of the intersection of 17th
Street and Pennsylvania Avenue (4.2 miles); Federal Triangle,
on 12th Street (3.4 miles); and Smithsonian, on the Mall at
12th Street (3.1 miles). Also, you can take a short cut to the
end of the hike by walking two blocks south from the
intersection of East Capitol and 1st Streets (1.3 miles) to the
Capitol South station.

Places to Stop for a Rest

Convenient rest stops are: Constitution Gardens (7.7 miles),
the District of Columbia World War I memorial (6.8 miles),
the Tidal Basin (6.6 to 5.8 miles), the Ellipse (4.8 to 4.6
miles), Pershing Park (3.8- miles), the Mall east of 12th Street
(3.1 to 2.4 miles), the grotto on the Capitol grounds (2.0-
miles), the west terrace of the Capitol (1.8 miles), and Stewart
Square (0.6 miles).

Places to Stop and Eat

The first place you can get food and drink on this hike is the
small refreshment stand next to the Washington Monument
along 15th Street (5.2 miles). There are a few upscale
restaurants along Pennsylvania Avenue (3.8- to 3.4 miles),
including a good one in the magnificently restored Willard
Hotel that offers light meals at <u>relatively</u> reasonable prices.

One of the best places for food on this hike is the pavilion of the Old Post Office Building (3.4 miles), with its many restaurants and food stands. Most of the museums and galleries on the Mall (3.1 to 2.4 miles) have places to eat at reasonable prices. Last, near the end of the hike along Pennsylvania Avenue S.E. (0.5 miles), is a string of bars and restaurants.

Public Rest Rooms

This hike is blessed with many public rest rooms well distributed along the route: the Lincoln Memorial (8.0 miles), on the Mall near the District of Columbia World War I memorial (6.8 miles), the refreshment stand next to the Washington Monument along 15th Street (5.2 miles), the Old Post Office Building (3.4 miles), and any of the museums and galleries on the Mall (3.1 to 2.4 miles). In addition, most of the government buildings along the route of the hike have rest rooms available to the public.

Some Cautions

This is a long hike and it can be arduous, particularly during Washington's hot, humid summers. You may, therefore, want to consider using one of the intermediate Metro stations (see above) to divide the hike into a two-day outing. Also, in hot weather, take advantage of the many air-conditioned public buildings along the route to get a break from the heat.

On-Route Directions After You Start

Numbers in the left margin indicate miles to the end of the hike. Unless otherwise indicated, maps are oriented north to top of page.

9.0   After you pass through the fare card machines at Arlington Cemetery Metro station, you have a choice of two exits that lead up to street level. Take the exit on your left. When you reach street level at the top of the escalator, you are facing west toward the formal marble entrance to Arlington National Cemetery, with Memorial Bridge, the Lincoln Memorial, and the Washington Monument at your back. Make a U-turn to the right and walk east toward Memorial Bridge.

8.8   At a traffic circle before Memorial Bridge, turn to
        the right and walk counterclockwise half way around
        the circle and then onto the bridge. (CAUTION:
        Before you come to the bridge, you must cross a
        highway with fast-moving traffic coming from your
        right. There is a crosswalk here but few motorists
        pay any attention.)

        *While you are crossing Memorial Bridge, directly
        ahead of you is the Lincoln Memorial. In the far
        distance to the right (south) of the Lincoln Memorial
        are the Romanesque tower of the Old Post Office
        Building, the Washington Monument, the Capitol, and
        the Jefferson Memorial, all of which you will pass later
        in this hike. Looking up the Potomac to the left (north)
        of Lincoln Memorial, are the small white dome of the
        Old Naval Observatory, the white marble Kennedy
        Center for the Performing Arts, with its narrow gilt
        columns, and, in the distance on the hill, the Gothic
        towers of the Washington National Cathedral.*

        *On weekdays there are normally many joggers on
        Memorial Bridge. These are largely service men and
        women working at the Pentagon who are required to
        keep themselves physically fit. The Pentagon is in
        Virginia about a mile to the south.*

8.3   At the other end of Memorial Bridge, bear to the
        right and walk counterclockwise around the traffic
        circle that encloses the Lincoln Memorial.
        (CAUTION: When crossing the first two crosswalks
        on the circle, be careful of the fast-moving traffic
        coming off the bridge behind you.)

8.0   About half way around the circle, cross to the inside
        and walk up the steps to the Lincoln Memorial.
        There are public rest rooms and drinking fountains
        on the left side of these steps. (See Map 7-1.)

        *The white marble Lincoln Memorial has many
        similarities to a classical Greek temple. It was
        dedicated in 1922 on a site that not too many years
        before had been part of the Potomac River. From the
        top of the steps, looking east across the Mall, you can
        see the Washington Monument and, directly behind it,
        the Capitol. Later in the hike you will have the
        opportunity to view the Mall from the opposite*

direction while standing on the west side of the Capitol. The copper dome just to the right of the Capitol is the Library of Congress, and the "castle" tower just to the right of that is the original Smithsonian Institution building.

The steps of the Lincoln Memorial are sacred in the history of American civil rights. It was here on Easter Sunday 1939 that African American contralto Marian Anderson sang to an audience of 75,000 after being refused the use of the Daughters of the American Revolution Constitution Hall, the only large concert hall then in the city. It was also here that Dr. Martin Luther King, Jr., delivered his famous "I Have a Dream" oration before a crowd that filled the area around the monument and down both sides of the reflecting pool.

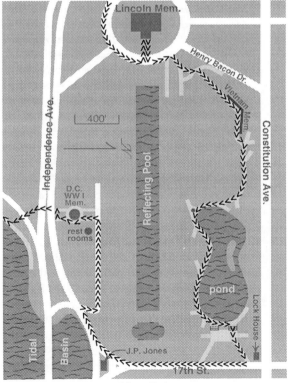

Map 7-1

8.0   After visiting the Lincoln Memorial, continue in the
        same direction (counterclockwise) around the circle.
        (See Map 7-1.)

8.0-   In a short distance, at the second path to your right
        (before reaching Henry Bacon Drive), turn right,
        away from the circle.   Follow the path, first to the
        left and then to the right, to the sunken black granite
        wall that constitutes the Vietnam Veterans Memorial.
        (See Map 7-1.)

7.9   Follow the path along the black granite wall. (See
        Map 7-1.)

        *Imprinted on the wall of the Vietnam Veterans
        Memorial are the names of the more than 58,000 men
        and women who died or are missing in the nation's
        longest and most controversial war. Like the war
        itself, the memorial's early history was controversial.
        Many thought the design by a 21-year-old Yale
        University student was too unconventional and not
        sufficiently uplifting. Since its dedication in 1982,
        however, the memorial has been judged by popular
        opinion to be a most moving and expressive site and
        has become a place of national mourning and
        reconciliation, the most visited of all Washington's
        monuments. Spontaneously, the friends and families of
        the fallen began to leave mementos at the base of the
        wall, mostly flowers but also touching articles like
        poems and childhood toys. The offerings have become
        so numerous that they are collected regularly by the
        National Park Service and placed in safe keeping.*

7.8   Upon leaving the black granite wall, follow the path
        as it turns to the left and then, in a short distance, at
        the first intersection of paths, keep to the right.
        From here on, continue to keep to the right on the
        path until you come to a large, peanut-shaped pond.
        (See Map 7-1.) The large street to your left here is
        Constitution Avenue.

7.7   When you reach the pond, follow the path to the
        right, along the southern side of the pond. (See Map
        7-1.)

        *The pond and surrounding area are known as
        Constitution Gardens. One of the more recent (1976)*

and long-anticipated improvements to the monumental part of the city, the gardens are on a site once occupied by "temporary" buildings erected here during World War I. The buildings not only outlasted that war, they became part of a larger complex of temporary buildings (including connecting walkways over the Reflecting Pool) that were crowded onto the mall during World War II. The need for these wartime buildings mostly disappeared with the end of World War II and the construction of the Pentagon in nearby Virginia. However, the World War I buildings were not torn down until 1971. The pond is now home to a variety of waterfowl, some of which no longer migrate to the north in summer as they should, presumably finding the handouts from summer tourists too tempting.

7.4   At the far (easternmost) end of the pond, there are two sets of steps leading up a terraced slope. Ascend the second, leftmost set. At the top of these steps, continue straight (east), across a small plaza area, onto a path that leads diagonally to the left. (See Map 7-1.)

7.3   Where the path comes to a large street (17th Street), turn right (south) onto the sidewalk along the right side of the street. (See Map 7-1.)

The small stone building to your left, just before you make the turn onto 17th Street, once served as a lockkeeper's house marking the eastern end of a canal that followed the bank of the Potomac River from this point back to Georgetown and the terminus of the C&O Canal. A little to the east of here, along the present alignment of Constitution Avenue, was the Washington City Canal, which for a while served the central part of the city. Built between 1810 and 1815, this canal fell into disuse and its slow-moving waters became mostly a fetid open sewer. The canal was covered over in the late 19th century, its stench lying hidden, only to be uncovered during Metro subway construction nearly a century later.

As you walk down 17th Street, the Washington Monument is to your left, rising from the top of a small hill. The east bank of the Potomac once passed just under this hill.   The land presently extending from there west to Memorial Bridge and south of Constitution Avenue was reclaimed from the river in the late 19th century.   The Washington Monument itself stands 555 feet tall and is the world's tallest pure masonry structure.   The cornerstone was laid in 1848, but since there was no steady source of funds, work continued only sporadically and the monument was not completed until 1884.   The change in the color of the monument's marble, about one-third of the way up from the base, marks a 17-year period beginning in 1859 when work stopped completely.

7.1   Continue to follow 17th Street as its right lanes turn gradually to the right. (See Map 7-1.)

To your left across the right lanes of 17th Street stands a statue of John Paul Jones (1747-92), Revolutionary War naval hero, known best perhaps for his response to an enemy demand that he strike his colors, "I have not yet begun to fight!"

7.0   A short distance after passing the John Paul Jones statue, turn sharply to the right onto a small, unmarked blacktop road with an iron chain along one side. (See Map 7-1.)

7.0- In a short distance, continue to follow the road as it turns sharply to the left (west). (See Map 7-1.)

The open area to the right of the road that is now used as athletic fields was the site of "Resurrection City." In the spring of 1968, three thousand poor people camped here in a makeshift canvas and plywood city. Organizers of the encampment, including the Reverend Ralph David Abernathy (successor to the just-assassinated Dr. Martin Luther King, Jr., as head of the civil rights organization known as the Southern Christian Leadership Conference) vowed to stay there until   Congress   passed   sweeping   anti-poverty legislation.   However,   bad   weather   and   some controversial incidents with the police led to the camp's closing in less than two months.

6.8   A short distance after passing a small circular building on your left containing rest rooms, turn to

the left (south) toward a round, columned, white
marble monument. (See Map 7-1.)

*The monument is a memorial to citizens of the District
of Columbia who served in the armed forces during
World War I. Its classical, symmetric design and
peaceful, wooded surroundings are reminders of a
simpler and quieter past and are in high contrast to the
angular, black granite Vietnam Veterans Memorial.*

6.7   Continue in the same direction past the monument to
        a divided, six-lane roadway. This is Independence
        Avenue. Cross the avenue at a crosswalk a short
        distance to the right (west). (See Map 7-1.)

6.7-   After crossing Independence Avenue, continue
        straight ahead on a walkway. In a short distance,
        cross a small road and then walk through the cherry
        trees to the edge of the Tidal Basin. (See Map 7-1.)

6.7-   At the Tidal Basin, turn right and follow the path
        along the water's edge. The path leads to the
        Jefferson Memorial, which is in plain view across
        the water.   (See Map 7-1.)

*The cherry trees ringing the Tidal Basin make a great
place to picnic. A gift from the Emperor of Japan, the
original trees were planted in 1912. Much to the
continuing dismay of the organizers of Washington's
annual Cherry Blossom Festival, the trees have an
almost perfect record of refusing to time their
blossoming to coincide with the scheduling of the
festival. The Tidal Basin, like the western end of the
Mall, was created from the Potomac through dredging
and land reclamation in the late 19th century.*

6.0   About two-thirds of the way to the Jefferson
        Memorial, follow the path across a stone bridge.

6.0-   On the other side of the bridge, continue on the path
        to the left around the Basin.

*Directly ahead after crossing the bridge you can see a
small, circular garden with a lily pond. This lovely
spot is worth the short detour to visit.*

5.8   Arrive at the Jefferson Memorial.

The Memorial was dedicated by President Franklin Roosevelt on June 13, 1943, the 200th anniversary of Jefferson's birth. However, the bronze statue of Jefferson was not placed in the monument until the metal shortages of World War II had ended. Initial construction of the monument, begun before World War II, was complicated by protesters who chained themselves to the cherry trees that would have to be removed. The monument stands on reclaimed land and is placed along an exact north-south axis with the White House. If you stand on the top steps of the monument you can see the White House directly to the north across the Mall.

5.8   To resume the hike after visiting the Jefferson Memorial, continue in the same direction on the path along Tidal Basin.

5.6   Follow the path across another bridge. (See Map 7-2.)

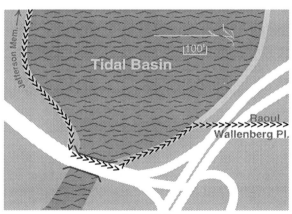

Map 7-2

5.6-   On the other side of the bridge, turn to the left, away from the road, back onto the path along the edge of the Tidal Basin. (See Map 7-2.)

5.5   At the first path leading to the right away from the Tidal Basin (before reaching the floating boat docks), turn right and, in a few steps, at a traffic-light controlled-intersection, continue straight (north)

across a divided road onto Raoul Wallenberg Place.
(See Map 7-2.)

The first large government building on the opposite side of Raoul Wallenberg Place is the Bureau of Engraving and Printing, where U.S. paper money and postage stamps are printed.

Just past (to the north of) the Bureau of Engraving and Printing (also on the opposite side of Raoul Wallenberg Place) is the U.S. Holocaust Museum honoring both victims and survivors of the Nazi death camps. Raoul Wallenberg, for whom the street is named, was a Swedish diplomat who saved many potential Holocaust victims. Wallenberg disappeared at the end of World War II and is believed to have been murdered by the Soviet secret police after refusing to act as a Soviet agent.

5.2   In one long block, where Raoul Wallenberg Place crosses Independence Avenue (unmarked the last time I passed here) and becomes 15th Street, continue straight (north) and follow 15th as it winds across the Mall, leaving the Washington Monument to your left. (NOTE: About halfway across the Mall stands a small building with a souvenir shop in front, public rest rooms on the sides, and a refreshment stand in back.)

4.9   On the other side of the Mall, where 15th Street intersects Constitution Avenue, cross and then turn left (west) onto Constitution Avenue. (See Map 7-3.)

4.9-   After walking a few steps on Constitution Avenue west of 15th Street, turn right and follow the sidewalk along the right side of a small unmarked road. (See Map 7-3.)

To your right, just after making the above turn, is a small stone building that once served as a gatehouse on the Capitol grounds. Known as the Bulfinch Gatehouse, after the architect Charles Bulfinch who completed reconstruction of the Capitol after it was burned by the British during the War of 1812, the building was moved here around 1874 when the

*Capitol grounds were redesigned by the famous
landscape architect Frederick Law Olmsted. You will
pass some of Olmsted's work later in the hike. There
is a notch in the stone of the gate house showing the
high-water mark of one of Washington's worst floods.
Water reached this level on February 12, 1881, when,
after massive rains and a sudden thaw, jammed ice
floes created a dam across the Potomac at Long
Bridge, about a mile downriver from here. Floodwater
covered much of the Mall and Pennsylvania Avenue.*

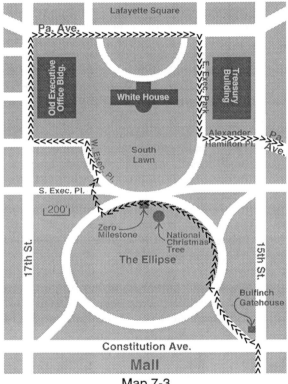

Map 7-3

4.8   At the first intersection, cross the intersecting road
        and turn right onto the sidewalk. The road should
        now be to your right and a large open grass field to
        your left. (See Map 7-3.)

        *The curved road you are now following encloses a
        park area to your left called the Ellipse. Perhaps best
        known as the location of the National Christmas Tree,
        the Ellipse has been used since the Civil War for*

baseball games and other athletic events. Also, during summer evenings, the U.S. Army stages elaborate displays of military ceremony here for special guests and the public.

4.6   About one-third of the way around the Ellipse, after passing the National Christmas Tree on your left, you come to the Zero Milestone (in the middle of the sidewalk) and the classic view of the South Lawn of the White House to your right. (See Map 7-3.)

The Zero Milestone is the reference point for measuring distances to and from Washington.

The South Lawn is technically the back yard of the White House, although the formal diplomatic entrance of the building faces this direction. The South Lawn is where the president and important guests arrive and depart by helicopter. Overlooking the back yard is a back porch -- the second-story balcony that Harry Truman had built within the columns of the White House's south portico. The balcony created much controversy at the time among architects, historical purists, and Republicans but has since become a much-appreciated addition to the building.

4.5   A short distance after passing the Zero Milestone, where the low black iron fence on your right ends, turn to the right. Continue straight across three roads (the elliptical road, South Executive Place, and West Executive Place) toward the White House grounds. (See Map 7-3.)

4.5-   After crossing West Executive Place, turn left. The black iron fence surrounding the White House grounds should now be immediately to your right. (See Map 7-3.)

4.4   Where West Executive Place ends at its intersection with State Place, turn left (west) onto State Place. (See Map 7-3.)

On the right (north) side of State Place stands the ornate Old Executive Office Building. When it was finished in 1888, this was the world's largest office building. Originally it housed the Departments of

State, War, and Navy. It now holds a part of the Executive Office of the President. After World War II, the building was considered by many to be an architectural eyesore and was slated for demolition until it was saved and restored during the Kennedy Administration. Much of the interior of the building is made of cast iron forged on the site during its construction. Drilling through this cast iron has become a challenge to those installing the communications cables required by a modern government office.

Across State Place from the Old Executive Office Building, on your left as you walk along State Place, is a monument to the U.S. First Infantry Division, nicknamed "The Big Red 1." On the far side of the monument, a giant floral number "1" is laid in the grass.

4.3   In one block, at the intersection of State Place and 17th Street, turn right (north) onto 17th. (See Map 7-3.)

4.2   In one block, at the intersection of 17th and Pennsylvania Avenue, turn right (east) onto Pennsylvania. (See Map 7-3.) (NOTE: The Farragut West Metro station is two blocks north of Pennsylvania at 17th and I Streets. On weekends you must use the 18th and I Streets entrance.)

The redbrick Renwick Gallery on the northeast corner of 17th and Pennsylvania has public rest rooms and provides a good break from the heat on a hot day. The small gallery, which displays both permanent and temporary collections of art and fine crafts, was designed by James Renwick, architect of the old Smithsonian Building and other Washington landmarks. After visiting the gallery, re-cross Pennsylvania Avenue and turn to the left (east) so that you are walking down the right (south) side of the avenue.

Just past (to the east of) the Renwick Gallery, are Blair House and Lee House. Built in 1824 and 1859 respectively, the buildings were acquired by the government in the 1940s and have since served as guest houses for distinguished visitors to the White

House. President Truman and his family stayed in Blair House during a major White House renovation, and it was here, on November 1, 1950, that two Puerto Rican separatists attempted to assassinate the President.

Pennsylvania Avenue in front of the White House has been closed to vehicular traffic for security reasons since the bombing of the Oklahoma City federal building in April of 1995 and is now a pedestrian mall.

4.1   You reach the north entrance of the White House on your right. (See Map 7-3.)

The White House, appearing almost daily in the news, is one of the world's most recognizable buildings. When it was first occupied in 1800 by President John Adams and his wife Abigail, it was barely known outside the city. The building achieved its first brush with fame when it was put to the torch by the British in War of 1812. Painted white to mask the effects of the burning, it has been called the White House ever since. Throughout the 19th century it was little more than one of many large residences in Washington whose occupants regularly visited each other. The building has been modified and added to periodically and has undergone major renovation twice -- first courtesy of the British in 1814 and next, after decades of serious deterioration, during the Truman administration.

To your left, across Pennsylvania Avenue from the White House, is Lafayette Square, named for the French hero of the American Revolutionary War. Statues of foreign military leaders who took the American part in the war, including Lafayette, are set in each of the corners of the square. Originally planned as part of the White House grounds, the square is today famous as a site for organized and individual protests of every kind.

4.0   Immediately after passing the White House grounds, where the black iron fence ends, turn right (south) though a set of iron gates onto a wide pedestrian walkway that follows the east side of the White House grounds. The walkway is called East Executive Park. (See Map 7-3.)

The Greek revival building to your left houses the Department of the Treasury. Built between 1836 and 1869, it is one of the oldest federal buildings in the city. The location of the building, selected after much talk and delay, violates Pierre L'Enfant's original plan for the city. That plan would have allowed you to see the Capitol down Pennsylvania Avenue from the White House.

3.8   After passing through another set of iron gates, at the intersection of East Executive Park and Alexander Hamilton Place, turn left and walk down the left side of Alexander Hamilton Place. (See Map 7-3.)

The statue to your left on the south side of the Treasury Building is, not surprisingly, that of Alexander Hamilton, the first secretary of the treasury. The statue across the street to your right is of the Civil War hero or villain (depending on your historical allegiances) William Tecumseh Sherman.

3.8-   In one block, at the intersection of Alexander Hamilton Place and 15th Street, cross 15th Street and walk slightly to the right (southeast) down the left side of Pennsylvania Avenue. (See Map 7-3.)

The park on the southeast corner of Pennsylvania Avenue and 15th Street has benches, tables, and a refreshment stand. It also contains a statue and memorial to General John J. Pershing, leader of the American Expeditionary Force in France during World War I.

As you start down Pennsylvania Avenue, with the view of the Capitol in the distance ahead of you, you can see the grand design of the avenue.

Toward the end of the first block, on the left side of Pennsylvania Avenue, is the Willard Intercontinental Hotel. This is one of the city's grandest hotels. The present structure was built from 1901 to 1904 on the site of the smaller but even more famous Willard Hotel. Julia Ward Howe composed the "Battle Hymn of the Republic" while staying at this older hotel. It was a tradition for many years for the president-elect to stay at the Willard the night before his inauguration. It is said that General Ulysses Grant coined the term "lobbyist" from the influence seekers who regularly approached him in the lobby while he was staying at the hotel. The present hotel was opulently restored in the late 1980s. If you have a moment, step into the lobby and take a look at some of the results of the restoration.

3.7   In one block, at the intersection of Pennsylvania Avenue and 14th Street, cross 14th Street and turn slightly to the left (east) onto E Street.

In the middle of the block on E Street, on your left, stands the National Theater. The present structure was built in 1922, but the first National Theater was established on the site in 1835. For many years in the 19th century, this and Ford's Theater were the leading theaters in town. Except for a last-minute change in plans, Lincoln would have come here rather than to Ford's Theater on the evening of his assassination. His assassin, John Wilkes Boothe was, in fact, waiting for him at the National and had to make a last minute change in plan of his own.

The open space across E Street from the National Theater is called Freedom Plaza and is a favorite spot for skateboarders. The statue at the far (eastern) end is of General Casimir Pulaski (1747-1779), Polish patriot and hero of the American Revolutionary War.

3.5   In one block, at the intersection of E and 13th Streets, cross and then turn right (south) onto 13th.

3.5-   In one short block, at the intersection of 13th Street and Pennsylvania Avenue, turn left (southeast) back onto Pennsylvania.

3.4   In one block at the intersection of Pennsylvania Avenue and 12th Street, cross and then turn right (south) onto 12th.

On the left (east) side of 12th Street, starting at Pennsylvania Avenue, is the towering -- by Washington standards -- gray stone Old Post Office Building. Completed in 1899, for years it served as the headquarters of the U.S. Postmaster General. In the past, its Romanesque style has been considered out of place among the uniformly neoclassical federal buildings that surround it. It is for many, however, a wonderful break from architectural monotony. Barely saved from demolition, the building was restored in the late 1970s, its interior converted to a pavilion with restaurants and many food shops, making it a perfect place to stop for lunch or a snack. If you have time, take the elevator to the top of the tower, where there is an excellent view of the city. When you leave the Old Post Office Building, continue south on 12th Street.

(NOTE: In the middle of the block between Pennsylvania and Constitution Avenues, on the right (west) side 12th Street, is the entrance to the Federal Triangle Metro station.)

3.2   At the next intersection, where 12th Street crosses Constitution Avenue and enters a tunnel under the Mall, cross Constitution and continue straight (south), along a small road that is just to the left (east) of the entrance to the tunnel.

You are now entering Smithsonian Institution territory. The building to your right (west) here is the Smithsonian's National Museum of American History. The building to your left (east) is the National Museum of Natural History. There are public rest rooms and drinking fountains in these buildings as well as in all the other museums and galleries on the Mall. Most of the museums and galleries also have places to eat.

3.1   In one block, continue straight (south) across Madison Drive (unmarked the last time I passed this way), onto a gravel path crossing the Mall.

(NOTE: The Smithsonian Metro station is on the Mall just ahead of you and to the right.)

3.0   In the middle of the Mall are two wide gravel paths running east and west. Turn left (east) onto the second (the southernmost) of these paths. You should now be walking toward the Capitol, with a wide expanse of lawn to your left.

The first building on your right as you walk east on the Mall is the Freer Gallery, displaying an eclectic mixture of Asian and American art, including the

Peacock Room. This room was originally in the mansion of a wealthy Englishman who had it designed and decorated with the finest materials specifically to display a painting he had acquired from the expatriate American artist James McNeill Whistler. Whistler, however, was not satisfied with the setting and persuaded the owner to allow him to make a few changes. When the artist had finished his changes, the owner was horrified to discover that the room's finely tooled leather walls had been painted over with artistic graffiti -- huge gold peacocks. In art, what is at first considered horrid in time often becomes highly valued, and the builders of the Freer bought the room together with its painting and had them permanently installed in the gallery.

East of the Freer Gallery is the original Smithsonian Building, known affectionately as "the Castle." The building was designed by James Renwick and built between 1845 and 1855 with funds provided by the estate of James Smithson, a wealthy Englishman who admired but never visited the United States. Smithson's tomb is just inside the door. Also in the building are models showing the history of city planning in Washington. The models cover much of the route of this hike.

Behind the Smithsonian Building are the Institution's two newest museums, the National Museum of African Art and the Sackler Gallery of Asian Art. Besides their superb exhibits, they have the perhaps unique distinction among the world's major museums of being located completely underground.

East of the Smithsonian Building is the Arts and Industries building, which displays a wonderful selection of the exhibits from the 1876 American Centennial Exhibition in Philadelphia.

East of the Arts and Industries Building is the round Hirshhorn Gallery and, in a pit on its north side, the Gallery's open-air sculpture garden.

2.7   Cross 7th Street (unmarked when I was last here) and continue east toward the Capitol on the same path.

The large building on your right after you cross 7th Street is the National Air and Space Museum and opposite it, on the north side of the Mall, is the National Gallery of Art.

2.5   Cross 4th Street (unmarked when I was last here) and continue east toward the Capitol on the same path.

The angular modern building on the left (north) side of the Mall after you cross 4th Street is the East Building of the National Gallery of Art.

2.4   Cross 3rd Street (unmarked when I was last here) and continue east toward the Capitol on a blacktop path, to the edge of the Capitol Reflecting Pool.

2.3   At the edge of the pool, turn right (south) and walk halfway around the it. (See Map 7-4.)

The glass-roofed building to the south of the pool is the U.S. Botanic Garden.

2.1   On the opposite (east) side of the reflecting pool, at the Ulysses S. Grant Memorial, turn right (east) toward the Capitol past the statue of Grant and between the gloriously animated sculptures of horse-drawn artillery. (See Map 7-4.)

2.1-   Immediately past the Grant Memorial, turn left (north) onto the road (1st Street) that runs between the Grant Memorial and the Capitol grounds. (See Map 7-4.)

2.1-   In a short distance, where 1st Street intersects Pennsylvania Avenue at a small traffic circle, cross 1st and continue walking north on the other side of the street. The Capitol grounds should now be immediately to your right. (See Map 7-4.)

2.1-   In a short distance, after passing one entrance into the Capitol grounds, turn right and enter the grounds on a path. In a few steps, the path branches; take the branch to the right. (See Map 7-4.)

2.0   After short distance, upon reaching a small stone tower on your left, turn left onto another path. (See Map 7-4.)

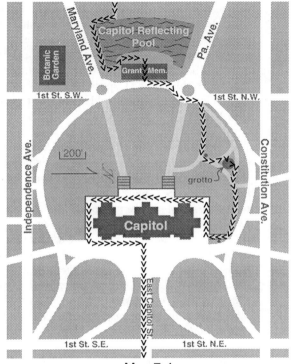

Map 7-4

2.0-   In a short distance, where the path branches, take the branch to the left and then, in a few steps, turn to the right and enter the small grotto. (See Map 7-4.)

> _Built in 1879, this secluded and little-visited grotto is one of the little masterpieces of Frederick Law Olmsted's complete redesign of the Capitol grounds. Olmsted is widely recognized as the father of American landscape architecture. His High Victorian design for the grounds makes for a wonderful contrast to the neoclassical Capitol._

2.0-   There are two entrances to the grotto other than the one through which you entered. Leave the grotto by the one to the left and make an immediate turn to the right onto a path that leads around the north end of

the Capitol. You should be walking in a direction
that puts the Capitol to your right. (See Map 7-4.)

1.8   Where the path comes together with the road to the
        left, just before reaching a small guard house, bear to
        the right onto a walkway that leads up a short set of
        steps onto a large balustrade-edged terrace. You are
        now at the northeast corner of the Capitol. Turn
        right and follow the terrace along the north, west,
        then south sides of the Capitol. As you walk around
        the terrace, the Capitol should always be to your left.
        (See Map 7-4.)

        *The cornerstone of the Capitol was laid in 1793 by
        George Washington. Despite many complaints about
        the muddy, mosquito-infested new city on the banks of
        the Potomac, the Congress moved here in 1800 to meet
        for the first time in the new building. Since then the
        building has undergone many modifications and
        renovations, including a rebuilding after it was burned
        by the British in 1814. The Capitol did not reach its
        present form until 1865, when the iron dome, built
        during the Civil War, was completed. For the
        etymologically curious, the name "Capitol" comes
        from "Capitolium," the temple to Jupiter on Capitoline
        Hill in ancient Rome.*

        *When you reach the west front of the Capitol, before
        you stretches a magnificent view of the monumental
        city -- much of which you have walked through on this
        hike. Directly in front of you, down the Mall, is the
        Washington Monument and, behind it, the Lincoln
        Memorial. The Mall divides the huge northwest
        quadrant of the city, to your right, from the vestigial
        southwest quadrant, to your left. Pennsylvania Avenue
        leads away diagonally to your right (northwest) to the
        Treasury Building and, hidden behind it, the White
        House. The street leading symmetrically to your left
        (southwest) is Maryland Avenue.*

1.5   Where the terrace ends at the southeast corner of the
        Capitol, turn to the left (north) and walk along the
        east front of the building. (See Map 7-4.)

1.4   When you reach the center of the east front, in the
        middle of the central set of steps, turn to the right

(east) and cross the plaza area on the crosswalk.
(See Map 7-4.)

1.4-   After crossing the plaza area, continue straight (east)
        from the crosswalk onto East Capitol Street
        (unmarked when I was last here). Follow the
        sidewalk on the right side of the street.
        (See Map 7-4.)

        (NOTE: East Capitol Street divides the northeast
        quadrant of the city to your left from the southeast
        quadrant to your right. The remainder of the hike
        passes through the southeast quadrant.)

1.3   At the intersection of East Capitol and 1st Streets,
        cross 1st and continue straight (east) along the right
        (south) side of East Capitol. (See Map 7-4.)

        (NOTE: The Capitol South Metro station is two
        blocks to your right (south) down 1st Street.)

        *The white marble building on your left after you cross
        1st Street is the Supreme Court. The gray stone
        building on your right is the Library of Congress. The
        entrance to the Library is half a block south on 1st
        Street. A quick visit to the magnificently ornate
        interior of the library is well worth a detour.*

        *On the right (south) side of East Capitol Street, after
        you cross 2nd Street, is the Folger Shakespeare
        Library. Inside the library is an actively used
        reproduction of an Elizabethan theater.*

        *The neighborhood you are entering as you walk along
        East Capitol Street is known as Capitol Hill. The
        name came from the hill, originally called Jenkins Hill,
        on the western edge of which the Capitol stands. Most
        of the townhouses around you were built in the late
        19th century and have been carefully restored by
        middle- and upper-income professionals, many of
        whom work for the Congress. But the area began as a
        working-class neighborhood populated largely by
        craftsmen working at two local industries. One was
        the construction and repeated reconstructions and
        restorations of the Capitol; the other was the
        Washington Navy Yard located about a mile to the*

south. The Navy Yard opened in 1799, six years after work had begun on the Capitol. At first the Navy Yard built ships, but later it shifted to armaments manufacturing and until the 1950s produced the Navy's largest guns.

0.9   At the intersection of East Capitol and 7th Streets, turn right (south) onto 7th.

0.7   In two blocks, just after you cross Independence Avenue, at the intersection of 7th Street and North Carolina Avenue, turn right (southwest) onto North Carolina Avenue. (See Map 7-5.)

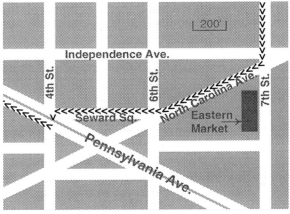

Map 7-5

The building on the southwest corner of 7th Street and North Carolina Avenue is the Eastern Market. Built in 1873 as one of the city's many fresh produce and meat markets, it continues to operate, offering a variety of culinary delights to satisfy the upscale tastes of today's Capitol Hill residents.

0.6   In one block, at the intersection of North Carolina Avenue and 6th Street, cross 6th and turn slightly to the right (west) onto Seward Square. (See Map 7-5.)

0.5   In two short blocks at the intersection of Seward Square, 4th Street, and Pennsylvania Avenue, cross and then turn right (northwest) onto Pennsylvania. (See Map 7-5.)

On the left (south) side of Pennsylvania Avenue, between 4th and 2nd Streets, is a commercial strip with a wide variety of restaurants and bars. You are just five short blocks from the end of the hike, making this is an excellent place to stop and reward yourself with a drink and maybe a meal. The bar conversation you overhear in these establishments will as likely as not be about politics.

0.3   At the intersection of Pennsylvania Avenue, 2nd Street, and Independence Avenue, cross 2nd and then turn half left (east) onto Independence.

Across Independence Avenue, to your right, is the Library of Congress building you passed earlier in the hike. The library's holdings, probably the largest in the world, require two annexes -- one, directly behind (to the east of) the original library, named the John Adams Building and the other, directly to your left, known as the James Madison Memorial Building. There is usually an exhibit of rare documents in the foyer of the Madison Building.

0.2   In one block, at the intersection of Independence Avenue and 1st Street, cross and then turn left (south) onto 1st.

0.0   In one block, just past the intersection of 1st and C Streets, you come to the Capitol South Metro station and the end of the hike.

NOTES

_____

_____

_____

_____

_____

_____

_____

_____

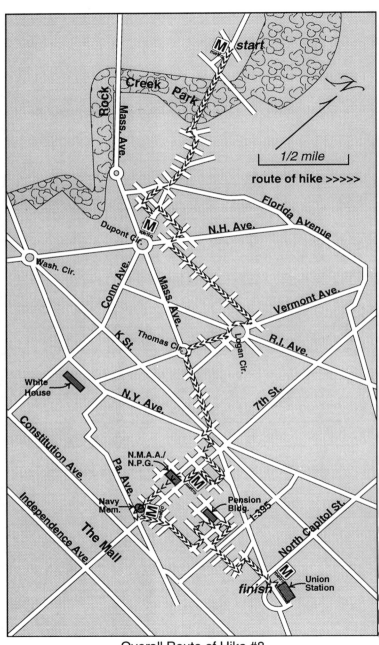

Overall Route of Hike #8
Woodley Park to Union Station

HIKE #8

The high-rent district; D.C.'s grand old neighborhood; the African American main street; Civil War heroes; an assassination conspiracy hideout among Chinese restaurants; synagogues, churches, and art galleries; the old commercial center; and a grand old railroad station.

From: Woodley Park Metro Station (D.C.)

To: Union Station Metro Station (D.C.)

Via: Connecticut Avenue, the Dupont Circle neighborhood, Q Street, Logan and Scott Circles, Massachusetts Avenue to Mount Vernon Square, Chinatown and the old downtown, the Navy Memorial, Indiana Avenue, and Judiciary Square.

Distance: 5.9 miles

Duration: 3 hours 20 minutes if you walk at 2.5 miles per hour and make six 10-minute stops.

Highlights

From the Woodley Park Metro station, the hike takes you south on Connecticut Avenue; across Rock Creek Park; past some luxurious old residential buildings; and into the Dupont Circle neighborhood, with its cosmopolitan atmosphere and its elegant old mansions. Hiking east on Q Street, you will cross 14th Street, once the "main street" of the city's vibrant majority African American community, and then turn south to Logan and Thomas Circles. You will then hike southeast from Thomas Circle on Massachusetts Avenue to Mount Vernon Square. Next you will meander south through the city's old commercial center -- past Chinatown and the old U.S. Patent Office turned art gallery -- and arrive at the Navy Memorial and the National Archives. From here you will go east on Indiana Avenue to Judiciary Square (site of the National Law Enforcement Officers Memorial) and the wonderful Victorian-era Pension Building, now home of the National Building Museum. Now you will go generally east -- past the miniature

Lillian and Albert Small Jewish Museum; the Italian Holy Rosary Church; and the Smithsonian Postal Museum -- and arrive at Union Station, restored to the splendor of the great days of railroading and enhanced with many modern shops and restaurants.

Things to Know Before You Start

All distances shown in parentheses below indicate miles to the end of the hike.

Intermediate Metro Stations

Metro stations located along the route of this hike are: Dupont Circle, one block south of the intersection of Hillyer Place and Connecticut Avenue (4.6 miles); Gallery Place-Chinatown (2.2 miles); Archives-Navy (1.7 miles); and Judiciary Square (1.0 miles).

Places to Stop for a Rest

Convenient rest stops along the route of this hike are: the small park at Connecticut Avenue and Kalorama Road (5.5 miles); Logan Circle (3.6 miles); the art galleries in the old U.S. Patent Office building (2.0 miles); the Navy Memorial (1.7 miles); and the Law Enforcement Officers Memorial (1.1 miles).

Places to Stop and Eat

A variety of restaurants can be found on both sides of Connecticut Avenue north and south of Hillyer Place (4.6 miles) and also along 17th Street north and south of Q Street (4.3 miles). There is, of course, a good selection of restaurants in Chinatown (2.3 miles). A small cafeteria is located in the old U.S. Patent Office building and, in good weather, you can sit in the building's lovely interior courtyard. Last, at the end of the hike, there are many restaurants and food shops within the restored elegance of Union Station (0.0 miles).

Public Rest Rooms

There are no public rest rooms in the first 3.9 miles of this hike. Farther on, you will find some at the following places:

the old U.S. Patent Office building (2.0), the Pension Building (1.1 miles), and Union Station at end of the hike (0.0 miles).

Some Cautions

The latter part of this hike threads its way through downtown streets that offer little shade and can be very hot on summer afternoons.

On-Route Directions After You Start

Numbers in the left margin indicate miles to the end of the hike. Unless otherwise indicated, maps are oriented north to top of page.

5.9   There is only one exit from the Woodley Park Metro station. When you reach street level on the escalator leaving the station, you are facing south, with Connecticut Avenue immediately to your left. Turn left and then immediately right and walk south on Connecticut. If you are walking in the right direction, the next cross street you come to will be Calvert Street.

5.7   Continue on Connecticut Avenue across the Taft Bridge high over the heavily wooded Rock Creek Park. (NOTE: At press time, Taft bridge was being repaired and you may have to cross Connecticut and use the sidewalk on the other side of the bridge.)

        Taft Bridge was built between 1897 and 1907. When it was completed, it was the largest unreinforced concrete bridge in the world.

        The drab tanbrick building on your right as you leave the bridge is the Chinese Embassy.

5.4   After leaving the bridge, follow Connecticut Avenue as it bears to the left. A safe way to do this is to walk around the tiny park in front of the Chinese Embassy, first to the right, then to the left onto Kalorama Road, and finally to the right back onto Connecticut. (See Map 8-1.)

        Connecticut Avenue is a boulevard of grand old apartment buildings, and the grandest of them all is _the tanbrick building to your left just south of Kalorama Road. Known as the "2102 Apartments," the large building contains only 66 units, each with a minimum of seven rooms. The building was built in 1928 and is a premier local example of art deco luxury._

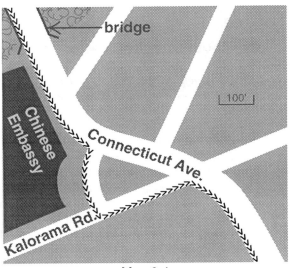

Map 8-1

In the block just south of Wyoming Avenue are the Embassies of Senegal, on the right, and Malta, on the left.

Farther down Connecticut Avenue on the left, just after you cross California Street, is the equestrian statue of General George McClellan -- commander of the Union Army of the Potomac during the Civil War, until he was removed by Lincoln after a long record of arrogance toward the President and inaction and timidity in the field. Believed by many to have been a Southern sympathizer, McClellan then ran unsuccessfully against Lincoln in the presidential campaign of 1864 on a platform of ending the war and letting the South go its own way. His statue is now condemned to look perpetually to the south over the city and directly toward the appropriately grand memorial to his nemesis and better, the martyred President.

4.9   At the intersection of Connecticut and Florida Avenues, continue in the same direction (south)

across Florida and then immediately cross and turn
right onto S Street. In a few steps, at the intersection
of S, Florida, and 21st, turn left (south) onto 21st.
(See Map 8-2.)

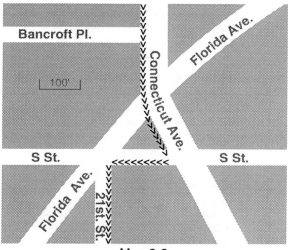

Map 8-2

Florida Avenue, previously called Boundary Avenue,
formed the northern boundary of the original
Washington City. The land north of the boundary was
part of the District of Columbia but was not
incorporated into the city until 1890.

4.7   In two blocks, at the intersection of 21st Street and
       Hillyer Place, turn left (east) onto Hillyer.

       The redbrick buildings on the right side of 21st Street,
       just south of Hillyer Place, house the fine collection of
       19th- and 20th-century paintings known as the Phillips
       Collection.

4.6   In one block, where Hillyer Place ends, turn left
       (north) back onto Connecticut Avenue. The last time
       I passed here there was a street sign at this corner
       indicating that the cross street is 20th Street. Ignore
       this sign -- 20th Street actually intersects
       Connecticut just to the south of this intersection.

       (NOTE: An entrance to the Dupont Circle Metro
       station is located one block south of Hillyer Place on
       Connecticut Avenue.)

This stretch of Connecticut Avenue is known for its bookstores, specialty shops, bars, and small restaurants. The stores and surrounding neighborhood were developed during the late 19th and early 20th centuries as part of an elegant residential area centered on Dupont Circle (two blocks south down the Connecticut). Although most of the larger houses have been converted to apartments or institutional headquarters, the faces of most of the buildings remain relatively unchanged. The neighborhood is included in the National Register of Historic Places and its character is protected by an active citizens association.

4.6-   In one block, at the intersection of Connecticut Avenue and R Street, turn right (east), cross Connecticut, and follow R to the east.

The redbrick-and-stone Renaissance-style building to your left just after you cross 20th Street is one of the neighborhood's original mansions. Built in 1890 as a residence for a merchant named George Fraser, the mansion for the last few decades has been home to a succession of clubs and restaurants.

The small apartment building with the columned entrance on right side of R Street, in the first block after 20th Street (number 1904), was once a private residence rented by Adlai E. Stevenson, the Democratic Party nominee for President who ran against Dwight Eisenhower in both the 1952 and 1956 presidential elections.

On the left side of R Street, just before 18th Street, is the National Museum of American Jewish Military History. Chartered by act of Congress in 1958, the museum commemorates Jewish Americans who have served in the U.S. armed forces in time of war. The museum is open weekdays from 9:00 am to 5:00 pm and Sundays from 1:00 to 5:00 pm. Mostly by coincidence, this hike passes a number of other important Jewish landmarks in the city.

4.4   At the intersection of R and 18th Streets, turn right (south) onto 18th. (When I was last here, there was no street sign for 18th.)

4.3   Just after crossing New Hampshire Avenue, at the
         intersection of 18th and Q Streets, turn left (east)
         onto Q.

         (NOTE: If you are in the mood for refreshments at
         this time, you will find a variety of restaurants along
         17th Street to the left and right of Q.)

         The tall building at 1615 Q Street, with the ornate,
         Near-Eastern-style entranceway, is the Cairo. Built in
         1894 as a swanky residential hotel, it soon gained a
         reputation for having residents who were wild and
         risque. However, by the middle of the 20th century,
         the building had became dilapidated and was barely
         saved from demolition. It has now been restored and
         converted to condominiums.

         When you cross 14th Street, you are crossing what was
         once the African American "main street" of
         Washington. Until the riots of 1968 following Martin
         Luther King's assassination, 14th Street was a thriving
         commercial strip and the location of some of the most
         important black-owned businesses in the city. The
         strip has slowly recovered from the riots and in the
         process has taken on a new identity. Among other
         things, it is now a center for small, experimental
         theater companies.

3.7   At the intersection of Q and 13th Streets, turn right
         (south) onto 13th.

3.6   In one short block, where 13th Street intersects
         Logan Circle, walk to the right (counterclockwise)
         around the circle.

         The neighborhood centered on Logan Circle was
         developed during the last quarter of the 19th century
         and is today the most purely Victorian part of the city.
         At first the neighborhood's makeup was solidly middle-
         class white. But then, around the turn of the century,
         when improved transportation made it practical and
         popular to live farther from the center of the city,
         Logan Circle slowly lost its white population and
         became solidly middle-class black. The area remained
         so until after World War II, when the Supreme Court's
         overturning of restrictive covenants made it possible

for affluent blacks to move farther out as well. The area then fell onto hard times, until, beginning in 1960s, middle-class professionals, both black and white, began the restoration of the fine old houses.

The equestrian statue at the center of the circle is of John A. Logan. Logan was a congressman from Illinois at the beginning of the Civil War who resigned his seat to joint the Union army. There he rose to the rank of major general. After the war he served as both congressman and senator.

3.5 A little less than half way around Logan Circle, turn right (southwest) onto Vermont Avenue.

On the right side of Vermont Avenue, in the first block, is the row house home of the National Council of Negro Women and the Bethune Museum - Archives. Until her death in 1955, this was the home and workplace of Mary McLeod Bethune -- founder of the Council and an important figure in national politics. During the 1930s, as a member of the so-called "Black Cabinet," she helped shape and promote Franklin Roosevelt's New Deal. She held high-level posts in several administrations and is the founder of the county's first African American college for women -- Cookman College in Florida (now called Bethune-Cookman College). The museum includes the National Archives of Black Women's History. The site is recorded in the National Register of Historic Places.

3.2 In two blocks, where Vermont Avenue intersects Thomas Circle, walk to the left (clockwise) around the circle.

The equestrian statue in the center of the circle is of Civil War general George H. Thomas. After his tenacious 1863 defense of Union Army lines along Chickamauga Creek in Tennessee, General Thomas came to be called "the Rock of Chickamauga."

3.2- About one-quarter of the way around Thomas Circle, just after you pass over the entrance to a highway tunnel under the circle, turn left (southeast) onto Massachusetts Avenue. You should now be walking down the right side of Massachusetts, and the next cross street should be 13th Street.

2.9   Where 11th Street crosses Massachusetts Avenue,
        there is no crosswalk. To continue down
        Massachusetts, you must turn right onto 11th, then,
        in a few steps, cross and turn left on L Street. L then
        comes back to Massachusetts, where you make a half
        turn to the right.

        *Just after turning back onto Massachusetts Avenue
        from L Street, you can see the multi-figured monument
        to labor leader Samuel Gompers across the avenue.*

2.7   Where Massachusetts Avenue intersects 9th Street, at
        Mount Vernon Square, turn right (south) onto 9th.
        (See Map 8-3.)

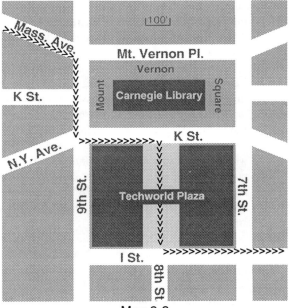

Map 8-3

2.7-   At the intersection of 9th Street with New York
        Avenue to the right and K Street to the left, continue
        straight (south) across New York, then turn left
        (east) across 9th and walk east along the right side of
        K. (See Map 8-3.)

        *The white marble building to your left across 9th
        Street, in Mount Vernon Square, was built in 1902
        (under an endowment from the steel magnate Andrew
        Carnegie) as the District of Columbia central library.*

The building has most recently been used by the University of the District of Columbia.

2.6   In half a block, turn right (south) onto a pedestrian walkway that passes under a large, glassed-in bridge connecting the buildings to the right and left. This is Techworld Plaza, and the pedestrian walkway is an extension of 8th Street. (See Map 8-3.)

The view south down 8th Street of the white-marble Greek revival old U.S. Patent Office building presents a striking contrast with the ultramodern buildings of the Techworld Plaza. You will visit the old Patent Office building later in the hike.

2.5   On the other side of the plaza, where the walkway intersects I Street, turn left (east) onto I . (See Map 8-3.) (The last time I was here there was no street sign for I Street.)

The church with a Byzantine-style dome and two towers, on the west side of 8th Street just below I, was once a synagogue, one of Washington's earliest. It is now the Greater New Hope Baptist Church. Interestingly, before there was a synagogue, the site was occupied by a Methodist Episcopal Church. That church building was bought by the Washington Hebrew Congregation in 1863 and used as a synagogue until it was replaced by the present structure in 1897.

2.4   In two blocks, at the intersection of I and 6th Streets, turn right (south) on 6th.

The multi-domed Turner Memorial African Methodist Episcopal Church, on the southwest corner of 6th and I Streets, was another early Washington synagogue. It too was built in the Byzantine style, which was the most popular architectural look for American Jewish houses of worship until well into the 20th century -- reflecting the prevalent style in the Holy Land, which remained under Turkish control until World War I. This temple was the second home of the Adas Israel Congregation. You will pass the original home of the congregation later in the hike.

2.3   In one block, at the intersection of 6th and H Streets, turn right (west) onto H.

The block of H Street between 6th and 7th Streets is the center of Washington's small Chinatown. An earlier Chinatown, dating back to the 1880s, was located to the south, along a short stretch of Pennsylvania Avenue. In 1931, when this older community was displaced by government office buildings, the Chinese businesses, organized through semi-clandestine associations called tongs, *moved as a group to the present site. The ornate Chinese archway over 7th Street is a recent addition, built jointly by the city governments of the District of Columbia and its "sister city" -- Beijing, China.*

Squarely within today's Chinatown is the pre-Civil-War-era building at 604 H Street, presently the Go Los Restaurant. This was once Mary Surratt's boarding house. It was here that the Lincoln assassination conspirators, led by John Wilkes Booth, met to plan the murder of the President and other top government officials. Mary Surratt, whose guilt or innocence has never been well established, was convicted and hanged as the only woman among the eight condemned conspirators.

2.2   At the intersection of H and 7th Streets, turn left (south) onto 7th. (An entrance to the Gallery Place-Chinatown Metro station is located on the southeast corner of 7th and H.)

(NOTE: As of presstime, a major sports arena was being planned for this neighborhood. Construction of this facility may require you to deviate from the specified route of the hike. If you get lost, ask for directions to the National Museum of American Art and when you arrive there continue the hike beginning at the direction marked 2.0 below.)

The row of buildings on your right, along the west side of 7th Street between H and G, shows what 7th Street looked like in the late 19th and early 20th centuries, when it was the most important mercantile street in the city. During Washington's early history, 7th Street had been an important commercial thoroughfare, connecting farms to the north with the Potomac River wharves to the south. Throughout most of the 19th century, the neighborhood was home to a mix of government employees and shopkeepers. As occurred around Logan Circle, late-19th-century transportation improvements drew these residents to new neighborhoods on the outskirts of the growing city, and they were replaced by successive waves of immigrants. In the decades before and after the turn of the century, 7th Street took on its predominant commercial role while becoming the center of a lively multiethnic neighborhood where lived mostly German and Jewish merchants and Irish and Italian workers. Gradually, as the middle years of the 20th century came and went, these residents, too, moved away and were replaced by African Americans, who, in their turn, followed the well-worn route outward if they could, leaving the neighborhood to its poorest black residents. The condition of the area reached its lowest point after the 1968 riots. More recently, a number of important public and private investments have led to a slow recovery.

2.1   In one block, at the intersection of 7th and G Streets, turn right (west) onto G. (See Map 8-4.)

The old U.S. Patent Office building should now be on your left occupying the block bounded by G and F Streets on the north and south and 7th and 9th Streets on east and west. The building was completed in 1867 and has served many functions through its history. Since 1968 it has been home to the Smithsonian Institution's National Museum of American Art and National Portrait Gallery. There are rest rooms in the building plus a small cafeteria with outside tables in the quiet interior courtyard.

2.0   Where 8th Street intersects G Street, to your right, turn left (south) across G and enter the National Museum of American Art (N.M.A.A.). After entering the building continue straight (south) through the interior courtyard and then through the National Portrait Gallery (N.P.G.), and exit the building on its south side. (See Map 8-4.) If the building is not open, walk around the outside of the building to its opposite (southside) entrance.

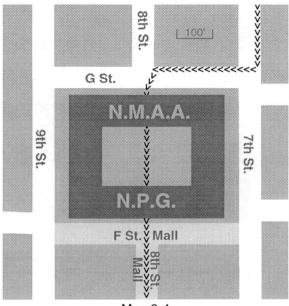

Map 8-4

2.0-   When you exit the National Portrait Gallery, walk
         straight (south), across the F Street pedestrian mall
         and down the 8th Street pedestrian mall. (See Map
         8-4.)

1.7   In two blocks, where 8th Street ends at its
         intersection with D Street, continue south between
         two matching buildings on another pedestrian mall to
         the circular plaza that makes up the Navy Memorial.
         (See Map 8-5.) (NOTE: The entrance to the
         Archives-Navy Memorial Metro station is just to the
         east of the memorial.)

         *The U.S. Navy Memorial honors Americans who have
         served in the Navy throughout the history of the
         country. In the center of the memorial is a huge map
         of the world laid into the "deck" of the site. A visitor's
         center in the building to the east provides additional
         information.*

1.7-   To resume the hike from the Navy Memorial,
         continue south a few steps to Pennsylvania Avenue
         and turn left, toward the Capitol, passing the
         equestrian statue of General Winfield Scott Hancock
         on your left. (See Map 8-5.)

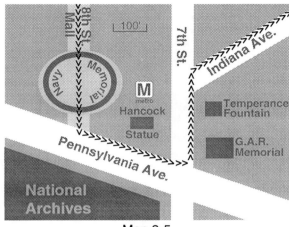

Map 8-5

Winfield Scott Hancock was a Union general during the Civil War and the Democratic Party's nominee for president in the election of 1880. He is perhaps best known for his role in the Battle of Gettysburg, where he commanded the Union troops on Cemetery Ridge that withstood the main force of Confederate General G. E. Pickett's fateful charge on July 3, 1863.

To your right, across Pennsylvania Avenue, is the National Archives building, home of the original Declaration of Independence, Constitution, and Bill of Rights. On this site, before the construction of the Archives in 1931, stood one of Washington's long-vanished and much-missed regional food markets, Center Market. The market first opened in 1801 and was rebuilt and expanded several times until, in the 1880s, it housed a thousand vendors' stalls and had space for three hundred wagons outside. Throughout its history it served as the city's most important source of fresh meat and produce.

1.6   In a short distance, at the intersection of Pennsylvania Avenue and 7th Street, cross and then turn left (north) onto 7th. (See Map 8-5.)

As you walk north on 7th Street you pass, on your right, the monument to the Grand Army of the Republic (an organization of Union army veterans) and the unusual and lovely Temperance fountain, one of many similar objects donated to American cities in the late

*19th century by a wealthy San Francisco dentist
named Henry Cogswell.*

1.6-   In one short block, at the intersection of 7th Street
        and Indiana Avenue, cross and then turn right
        (northeast) onto Indiana. (See Map 8-5.)

        *In the antique furniture store to your left, at 637
        Indiana Avenue, is probably the world's oldest
        operating safety elevator. The hand operated device,
        the product of inventor Elisha Graves Otis, was
        installed in the building in the 1850s. The building
        itself was built in 1826.*

1.4   In two blocks, where Indiana Avenue turns slightly
        to the right at its intersection with 5th and D Streets,
        turn half left and cross D, then turn right (east)
        across 5th and continue on Indiana to the east.

        *The Greek-revival building to your left as you walk
        east on Indiana Avenue currently serves as a D.C.
        Courthouse. Built between 1820 and 1849, it is one of
        the oldest public buildings in the city and at different
        times has served as City Hall, the U.S. Patent Office,
        and a Civil War hospital.*

1.3   In one block, at the intersection of Indiana Avenue
        and 4th Streets, turn left (north) onto 4th.

1.2   In one block, at the intersection of 4th and E Streets,
        cross and then turn left (west) onto E.

1.1   In half a block, turn right (north) and walk through a
        plaza (Judiciary Square) toward the large redbrick
        Pension Building.

        *In the center of Judiciary Square is the National Law
        Enforcement Officers Memorial. The memorial honors
        and lists the names of all the nation's law enforcement
        officers who have been killed in the line of duty.*

1.0   On the other side of Judiciary Square, just past the
        entrance to the Judiciary Square Metro station, turn
        right onto F Street. (When I was last here there was
        no sign for F Street.) The Pension Building should
        now be to your left across F.

Completed in 1882, the Pension Building is one of Washington's finest Victorian-era buildings. It was designed by Montgomery Meigs, engineer of the Capitol dome and chief Union army quartermaster during the Civil War. Built as a government office building, it has also served as the site of many presidential inaugural balls. Now it is home to the National Building Museum. The interior is spectacularly unusual for an office building and is worth stopping to see. Also, as you walk along the outside of the building, take note of the intricate frieze depicting Civil War scenes. There are public rest rooms in the building.

0.9   In half a block, at the intersection of F and 4th Streets, turn left (north) onto 4th.

0.9-   In one block, at the intersection of 4th and G Streets, cross and then turn right (east) onto G.

0.8   In one block, at the intersection of G and 3rd Streets, cross and then turn right (south) onto 3rd.

The small redbrick building on the northeast corner of 3rd and G Streets is the Lillian and Albert Small Jewish Museum, the second floor of which is the original sanctuary of Adas Israel congregation. The sanctuary was dedicated in 1876 and is the oldest synagogue built for that purpose in the city. The structure was originally located at 6th and G Streets N.W. and was moved to its present location in 1976 to save it from demolition.

The Holy Rosary Church, on your left in the first block of 3rd Street, is the only Italian church in the metropolitan area. Built in 1919, it was once the center of a small, thriving Italian-American neighborhood. The neighborhood declined with suburbanization after World War II and was finally decimated by the construction of the freeway that now cuts its way through the city just behind the church.

0.6   At the intersection of 3rd and E Streets, turn left (east) onto E and, in a short distance, cross over the I-395 freeway.

0.4   At the corner of E Street and New Jersey Avenue, cross and then turn left (northwest) onto New Jersey.

There is an unusual view of the Capitol to your rear as you walk up New Jersey Avenue.

0.3   In one block, at the intersection of New Jersey Avenue and F Street, turn right (east) onto F.

You are very near the end of the hike now, and, if you want to stop for a drink, there are two good Irish bars in this block of F Street.

0.1   Where F Street intersects North Capitol Street and Massachusetts Avenue, turn left (north) and cross F. Then turn right (east) across North Capitol, then left (north) across Massachusetts. Finally, turn right and walk southeast along the left side of Massachusetts.

The building on your left after you turn onto Massachusetts Avenue is the old central post office for D.C. The Smithsonian's postal museum is located in this building.

0.0   In one block, at the intersection of Massachusetts Avenue and 1st Street (N.E.), turn left onto 1st. In a few steps, turn right and cross 1st on a crosswalk to Union Station. The Union Station Metro station is located in the nearest (westernmost) end of the building. This is the end of the hike. There are public rest rooms and a wide variety of restaurants in Union Station.

Completed in 1908, Union Station replaced two earlier railroad passenger terminals, one located on the present site and the other located on the mall. Through the first half of the 20th century the huge station was the city's major point of entry and bustled with activity. Crowds have frequently gathered here for the arrival and departure of celebrities, including kings, queens, presidents, sports teams, and the Beatles. As rail travel declined after World War II, however, the status and condition of the station declined likewise. For a while a large part of the station had to be closed due to deterioration. Ultimate degradation came when it fell victim to a dreadfully inept and unfinished refurbishment carried out to convert it to a visitor's center for the hordes of tourists that were expected to descend upon the city in conjunction with the nation's bicentennial, in 1976. The hordes never came, and the desecrated building, which had been stripped of its function as a passenger terminal in favor of a slapdash Amtrak depot thrown up behind it, became a civic and bureaucratic nightmare. Rescue for the grand old station came in the form of a joint public-private venture to restore the building, re-establish and renovate its rail passenger facilities, and incorporate a 200,000 square-foot retail mall. The magnificently restored building opened in 1988 and has since been one of the city's most popular attractions.

NOTES

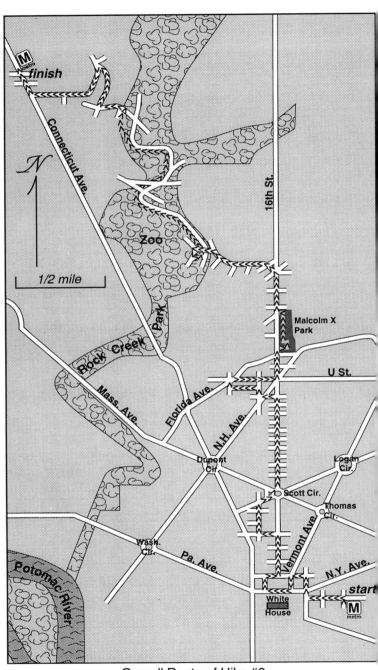

Overall Route of Hike #9
Metro Center to Van Ness

HIKE #9

**A walk through downtown; Revolutionary War
heroes; a trip through the lands of a real estate
empress; a stroll down a former African American
boulevard; a hike through the woods (with some
cliff hanging if you want); a water-powered grist
mill; and some exquisite gardens.**

From: Metro Center Metro Station (D.C.)

To: Van Ness Metro Station (D.C.)

Via: Downtown, Lafayette Square and the White
             House, 16th Street, the Strivers' Section and U
             Street, Malcolm X (Meridian Hill) Park, Rock
             Creek Park, Pierce Mill, and the Hillwood
             Gardens.

Distance: 6.5 miles

Duration: 4 hours if you walk at 2.5 miles per hour and
             make five 10-minute and one 30-minute stops.

Highlights

This hike begins in Washington's old downtown, still the
location of some of the area's largest offices and department
stores. From here you will walk west to the White House and
Lafayette Square, with its statues of Revolutionary War heroes
and its modern-day protesters. Hiking north, you will pass the
National Geographic Society, with its Explorers Hall, and
then a long string of fine old churches and mansions along
16th Street. From 16th you will make a side trip through the
Strivers' Section, once home to many of Washington's most
ambitious and successful African Americans. Returning to
16th Street by way of U Street, you will again hike north,
through the formal gardens of Malcolm X Park, and then
descend via Harvard Street into the heavily forested valley of
Rock Creek Park. After passing the entrance to the National
Zoo, you will hike north through the woods along the banks
of Rock Creek to Pierce Mill -- an operating, water-powered
grist mill. Now you will climb out of the valley, past the

lovely gardens at the Hillwood Museum to Connecticut Avenue and the end of the hike at Van Ness Street.

Things to Know Before You Start

All distances shown in parentheses below indicate miles to the end of the hike.

Intermediate Metro Stations

None.

Places to Stop for a Rest

Convenient rest stops along the route are: Lafayette Square (5.9 miles), Malcolm X Park (3.6- miles), Harvard Square (3.1 miles), the Zoo (2.5- miles), and the park just before you reach Pierce Mill (1.2 miles).

Places to Stop and Eat

Between P and R Streets (5.0- miles) on 17th Street are a number of small, reasonably priced restaurants. The Zoo (3.5- miles) has a few small restaurants and refreshment stands. Finally, at the end of the hike is a fair variety of restaurants along Connecticut Avenue near the Van Ness Metro station (0.0 miles).

Public Rest Rooms

Public rest rooms are located along the route of the hike at Lafayette Square (5.9 miles), the National Geographic Society Explorers Hall (5.0- miles), the Zoo (2.5- miles), and Rock Creek Park just before you reach Pierce Mill (1.2 miles).

On-Route Directions After You Start

Numbers in the left margin indicate miles to the end of the hike. Unless otherwise indicated, maps are oriented north to top of page.

6.5   Metro Center is a complex station with a number of exits. If you arrive at Metro Center by the blue or orange lines take one of the escalators or stairways leading up from the train platform to the upper, red line level. From the red line level, follow the signs

to 13th Street. These signs will lead you to the 13th
and G Streets exit. When you reach street level on
the escalator, make a U-turn to the right and follow
13th Street north. In a few steps, at the intersection
of 13th and G Streets, turn left (west) onto G.
(NOTE: If you get lost leaving Metro Center, ask for
directions to 13th and G and from that intersection
follow G west -- the direction of increasing street
and building numbers.)

*Metro Center is in the midst of the city's central retail
shopping area -- Washington's downtown. This was,
until thirty or forty years ago, the only major shopping
area in metropolitan Washington. Its grand
department stores and movie palaces attracted people
from all over the area. Today all but one of the
department stores have either vanished or moved to the
suburbs and the movie palaces have all been run out of
business by smaller neighborhood cinemas. But the
downtown struggles to survive. Revitalization began
with the building of Metro and has continued with
restoration of hotels and the building of a convention
center and new high-rent apartment buildings.*

*On the right (north) side of G Street between 13th and
14th Streets stands the Church of the Epiphany. The
church was built before the Civil War and for a time
during that war served as a makeshift surgical ward
for Union soldiers brought here after the disastrous
first Battle of Bull Run.*

6.2   In two blocks, at the intersection of G and 15th
Streets, turn right (north) onto 15th.

*The neoclassical building across 15th Street is the
Treasury Building -- one of the oldest government
buildings in the city.*

*The gloriously ornate redbrick structure on the
northeast corner of 15th Street and New York Avenue
is the National Savings and Trust Building. Built in
1888, it now houses a Crestar Bank.*

6.1   At the intersection of 15th and H Streets, turn left
(west) onto H.

During the latter part of the 19th century, the southwest corner of 15th and H Streets was occupied by the elegant and fashionable Wormley Hotel. Important people stayed at the hotel, and it was the site of much political drama, including the meeting that ended the 1876 presidential election stalemate between Rutherford B. Hayes and Samuel Tilden, in which the "party of Lincoln" betrayed the beleaguered freed slaves of the South by agreeing to end enforcement of Reconstruction with federal troops in exchange for southern Democrats agreeing to concede Hays the election. Ironically, the hotel's founder and proprietor was the adventurous and industrious James Wormley, an African American.

6.0   In one block, at the intersection of H Street and Madison Place, turn left (south) onto Madison.

The building on the southeast corner of H Street and Madison Place is known as the Cutts-Madison House. Built in 1820, it was originally owned by former president James Madison. When Madison died, his widow, Dolly, took up residence and lived here until her death in 1849. During the Civil War, the building served for a time as headquarters for the Army of the Potomac -- the principal Union army in the East. Still more recently, the National Aeronautics and Space Administration used the building as one of its early headquarters.

On the northeast corner of Madison Place and Pennsylvania Avenue once stood the Freedmen's Savings Bank. Organized in 1865, the bank was meant to provide banking services to freed slaves. For a number of reasons, including mismanagement and fraud, the bank collapsed in 1874, taking with it the life savings of thousands of depositors.

5.9   In one block, at the intersection of Madison Place and Pennsylvania Avenue, turn right, cross Madison, and walk west along Pennsylvania across the street from the White House.

The park on your right is Lafayette Square, honoring the Marquis de Lafayette, the French general who fought with the Americans in the Revolutionary War. The Marquis's statue stands in the southeast corner of the square. The other three corners are also occupied by foreign military officers who helped in the Revolutionary War. In the southwest corner is Jean de Rochambeau, commander of the French forces at the Battle of Yorktown. In the northwest corner stands the Prussian, Frederick Baron von Steuben, the person most responsible for training the Continental Army. In the northeast corner is the Pole, Thaddeus Kosciuszko. The center of the square is occupied by a statue of Andrew Jackson. During the 19th century, Lafayette Square was the center of the city's social life, with the White House on one side and the houses of leading citizens lining the other sides. Today the square is known mostly as a site of political protests.

5.8 In one block, at the intersection of Pennsylvania Avenue and Jackson Place, turn right (north) onto Jackson.

The 19th-century row houses on Jackson Place were restored as part of a general facelifting of Lafayette Square during the 1960s. Among the many notable people who once lived in these houses are Theodore Roosevelt and William Randolph Hearst. A lesser-known figure was Major Henry R. Rathbone, an aide to President Lincoln who was with the president in his box at Ford's Theater when John Wilkes Booth shot him.

At the end of the block on Jackson Place on the left stands Decatur House. Completed in 1818, the house was home to naval hero Commodore Steven Decatur until 1820, when he was killed in a duel with a disgruntled fellow officer. Later, ownership of the house passed to John Gadsby, a well-know innkeeper and notorious slave trader. During Gadsby's ownership, slaves were quartered and auctioned on the property.

5.7 In one block, at the intersection of Jackson Place and H Street, turn right (east) onto H.

5.6 Halfway down the north side of Lafayette Square, where 16th Street intersects H Street from the left, turn left (north) and walk up the left (west) side of 16th.

(NOTE: There are public rest rooms here on the
north side of Lafayette Square.)

*The building on the northwest corner of 16th and H
Streets is the elegant Hay-Adams Hotel.   The hotel
was built in 1927 on the site that had been occupied
since 1885 by the attached homes of John Hay and
Henry Adams.   John Hay was Lincoln's private
secretary and later became an elder statesman, with
stints as secretary of state under Presidents McKinley
and Theodore Roosevelt. Henry Adams -- grandson
of President John Quincy Adams -- was a well known
writer, historian, and, with Hay, leader of Washington
society.*

*Opposite the Hay-Adams Hotel on 16th Street is Saint
John's Episcopal Church. Completed in 1816, it is one
of the oldest churches in the city. .With a pew
permanently reserved for the incumbent president, it
is known as the "Church of the Presidents."*

*To your left as you cross K Street is Washington's
high-rise office building district. Compared to those of
most other large cities, however, the high-rise
buildings of Washington are rather puny things. The
city has strict building height limits to prevent private
buildings from overshadowing the capital's public
monuments.*

5.4   At the intersection of 16th and L Streets, turn left
        (west) onto L.

5.3   In one block, at the intersection of L and 17th
        Streets, turn right (north) onto 17th.

*The large building on the right (east) side of 17th
Street just before M Street houses the National
Geographic Society. The ground floor of the building
contains Explorers Hall -- a geographical museum and
exhibition. There are also public rest rooms on the
ground floor.*

*On the northeast corner of 17th and M Streets stands
the beautifully restored Sumner School. The school
was built in 1871-72 to serve African American
children. The building served this function and also
acted as headquarters of Washington's separate black*

school system until school segregation was abolished in the District of Columbia in 1954. The school was named for U.S. Senator Charles Sumner, an outspoken opponent of slavery before the Civil War and an equally outspoken supporter of equal rights for freed slaves after the war. Sumner is perhaps best known as the victim of a vicious caning he received in the Senate Chamber at the hands of a congressman from South Carolina after Sumner had delivered a speech critical of the representatives from that state.

5.1   At the intersection of 17th Street and Rhode Island Avenue, cross and then turn right (northeast) onto Rhode Island Avenue.

5.0   In one block, cross Bataan Street and follow Rhode Island Avenue as it turns gradually to the left. (See Map 9-1.)

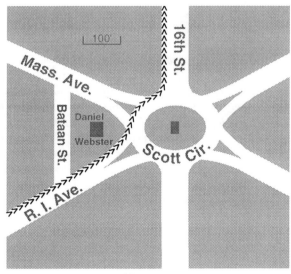

Map 9-1

5.0-   In a few steps, after passing a statue of Daniel Webster to your left, continue straight across both sides of the divided Massachusetts Avenue. Scott Circle will now be to your right. (See Map 9-1.)

The equestrian statue in the center of Scott Circle is of General Winfield Scott ("Old Fuss and Feathers"), hero of the Mexican War and commander-in-chief of

_the U.S. Army from 1841 to 1861, including briefly at
the start of the Civil War. The statue, cast from
captured and melted-down Mexican War cannon, was
the source of some controversy. It seems that by the
time the General posed for the statue he was too old,
fat, and frail to be seated on anything but a steady and
quiet mare. Much to the shock of Scott's friends and
admirers, the literal-minded sculptor produced a
statue with the General astride a mare. Since this
clearly would never do, the bronze horse subsequently
underwent a sex change operation._

5.0-   On the other side of Massachusetts Avenue, continue
       straight, leaving the Australian Embassy to your left,
       and then make a half turn to the left (north) onto
       16th Street. (See Map 9-1.)

       If, as you walk up 16th Street, you become interested
       in getting something to eat, there are a number of
       good and inexpensive restaurants one block to the
       west on 17th Street between P and R Streets.

       _Sixteenth Street is one of Washington's grand
       boulevards. The centerline of the street, which passes
       directly through the center of the White House, was for
       many years used as the prime meridian (the line of
       zero longitude) by the United States. Development
       along 16th Street began in the 1870s and produced
       some of the city's grandest residences. Many large
       churches were also built along the street -- so many, in
       fact, that the street is now commonly referred to as the
       "Street of Churches."_

4.4   At the intersection of 16th and T Streets, turn left
       (west) onto T.

4.3   After crossing New Hampshire Avenue, at the
       intersection of T and 17th Streets, cross and the turn
       right (north) onto 17th.

4.3-   In one short block, at the intersection of 17th and
       Willard Streets, turn left (west) onto Willard.

       _For the next few blocks you will be walking through
       the historic district known as the Strivers' Section.
       Originally developed as an all-white neighborhood at
       the eastern edge of the fashionable Dupont Circle_

district, the neighborhood turned black during the early 20th century. Soon it became known as the most prestigious place in the city for upwardly mobile African Americans to live.

4.1   In one long block, at the intersection of Willard and 18th Street, turn right (north) onto 18th.

4.1-   In one short block, where 18th Street intersects Florida Avenue, turn half right (northeast) onto Florida and then, in a few steps, turn half right (east) onto U Street.

This block of U Street was the center of the Strivers' Section and was lined with large, meticulously maintained row houses. U Street -- then a center of black commerce and nightlife -- was known in D.C.'s African American community as the "Black Broadway," a place where residents would parade in their finest dress after church on Sundays. Now sadly run down in some places, U Street declined rapidly with the end of racial segregation, when alternative places to live and shop were open to those African Americans who could afford them.

3.8   Where U Street intersects New Hampshire Avenue and 16th Street, turn left (north) back onto 16th.

3.6   Where 16th Street intersects Florida Avenue (to the east) and W Street (to the west), cross 16th and continue in the same direction (north) up the right (east) side of 16th.

Behind the red sandstone wall on the northwest corner of 16th Street and Florida Avenue once stood Henderson's Castle. The huge, ornate residence was built in 1888 by John B. Henderson and his wife Mary. Henderson was a Senator from Missouri and the author of the 13th Amendment, abolishing slavery. After locating on 16th Street, Mary became as well known locally as her husband. Until her death in 1931, she owned and developed many properties along 16th Street. Her tireless efforts to control and promote the area, including her effort to have the street renamed "Avenue of the Presidents," earned her the title of "Empress of 16th Street." Her castle was torn down in 1949 and the property redeveloped into middle-income townhouses in 1976.

3.6-   In a short distance, turn right (east), through the formal entrance into Malcolm X (formerly Meridian Hill) Park and continue east into the park a short distance to a large rectangular pool.

On the opposite side of the pool is a statue of James Buchanan, fifteenth president of the U.S.

3.5   From the left (north) side of the pool, ascend the steps (to the north) that parallel each side of a long water cascade. From the top of the cascade, ascend two flights of steps along a wall to the upper level of the park.

When you reach the upper level of the park, you will find a statue of Joan of Arc and a rare vista of the city to the south. In walking up the steps behind you, you have moved from the Coastal Plain, laid out before you, to the edge of the upland Piedmont that extends north and west to the Appalachian Mountains.

3.5-   To resume the hike on the upper level of the park, continue north (to the rear of the Joan of Arc statue) through the length of the park.

Meridian Hill Park was built by the city but was one of Mary Henderson's projects to enhance the area. Constructed between 1917 and 1936, it is probably the best-designed formal garden in the city. During the 1960s the park was used as an important rallying point for civil rights demonstrations, and it has since been renamed in honor of Malcolm X.

3.3   At the far (north) end of the park, turn left (west) and exit the park. Immediately on exiting the park, turn right and resume walking north up 16th Street.

3.3-   In a few steps, at the intersection of 16th and Euclid Streets, cross 16th and continue in the same direction (north) on the opposite side of 16th.

Two examples of the mansions built by Mary Henderson are at 2600 and 2633 16th Street. The first, on the northwest corner of 16th and Euclid, is now occupied by the Inter-American Defense Board and is sometimes called the "Pink Palace." The second, the large house with a cupola on the east side of 16th, is known as the Warder-Totten House. It was built largely from materials scavenged from an earlier house located in the 1500 block of K Street.

Within a short distance of Fuller Street, on 16th Street, are embassy buildings of Lithuania, Switzerland, Poland, Italy, Spain, and Mexico. The sign for the Swiss Embassy building is in Spanish because it presently houses the Cuban Interest Section -- the organization that officially acts for Cuba in the U.S. while there are no diplomatic relations between the two countries.

3.1   After crossing Fuller Street, make a half turn to the left (northwest) onto the first street (unmarked when I was last here) and, in a short distance, continue straight (northwest) across Columbia Road onto Harvard Street. (See Map 9-2.)

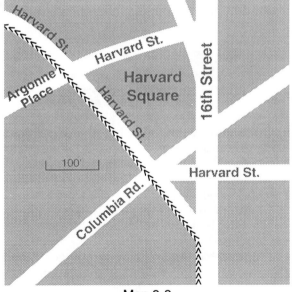

Map 9-2

To the right as you walk along Harvard Street is a small but well-used park called Harvard Square, with benches and drinking water. If you visit the park, you _are likely to hear a lot of Spanish, as this is one of the centers of Washington's Hispanic community._

3.0   After you pass Harvard Square, continue straight (northwest) on Harvard Street, across Argonne Place to your left, and down a hill. (See Map 9-2.)

2.6   At the bottom of the hill on Harvard Street, at an intersection with traffic lights, turn slightly to the left (leaving Harvard) and cross the bridge over Rock Creek into the National Zoological Park. (See Map 9-3.)

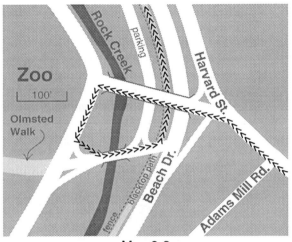

Map 9-3

2.5   On the other side of the bridge, at the intersection with an unmarked road, turn left without crossing the road. (See Map 9-3.)

2.5-   In a short distance, follow the sidewalk as it turns sharply to the left and, in a few steps, cross a small bridge back over Rock Creek. (See Map 9-3.)

        (NOTE: If, instead of making the above turn and crossing the second bridge, you continue straight and then turn right onto the large walkway (Olmsted Walk) leading into the Zoo, you will find rest rooms, drinking water, and a small cafeteria.)

2.5-   On the other side of the small bridge, leave the sidewalk and continue straight across a road on the left, pass through a fence gate, and turn left onto a blacktop path. (CAUTION: This path is heavily used by fast-moving bicyclists.) In a short distance, you walk under the bridge on which you first crossed Rock Creek. As you walk along the path here the fence enclosing the Zoo is immediately to your left and Beach Drive is immediately to your right. (See Map 9-3.)

Rock Creek meanders through a wooded stream valley from Maryland to the Potomac River near Georgetown. _The 2,100-acre stream valley was acquired by the federal government in 1890 to form Rock Creek Park._ _The surprisingly wild park, now home to foxes and deer as well as the usual opossums, raccoons, and birds, provides a wonderful escape from the heat and noise of the surrounding city._

1.9   In about half a mile, follow the blacktop path to the left across a bridge over Rock Creek. On the other side of the bridge, follow the path under a highway bridge and along the creek to your right.

1.8   In a short distance, where another blacktop path intersects from the left, bear to the right following the creek on your right under another highway bridge.

1.6   Follow the blacktop path to the right across a bridge back over Rock Creek and, on the other side, follow the path as it turns to the left.

Just before crossing the above bridge, there is a light-green-blazed dirt trail leading straight ahead into the woods. This is the Western Ridge Trail; it is an alternative, more secluded and beautiful route but also more difficult one -- being cut into a steep hillside. The Western Ridge Trail returns to the main blacktop path (called the Valley Trail) at direction 1.3 below. If you take the Western Ridge Trail, follow the light-green blazes carefully. (CAUTION: Do not take the Western Ridge Trail if you are not sure-footed, especially when the ground is wet or leaf strewn.)

1.3   Follow the blacktop path to the left across a bridge back over Rock Creek. On the other side of the bridge, where the blacktop path turns to the right, continue straight across a grassy field to a small building containing rest rooms. To your left here, the Western Ridge Trail emerges from the woods onto the grassy area (See Map 9-4.)

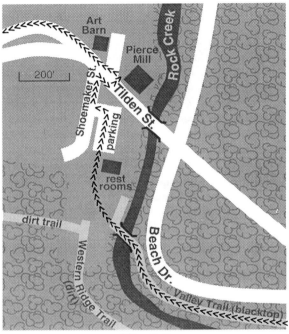

Map 9-4

1.2   Pass the rest rooms, leaving the building on your right. (See Map 9-4.)

1.2-   After passing the rest rooms, continue straight across a small parking area. (See Map 9-4.)

1.2-   In a short distance, at the far end of the parking area, turn left out of the parking area and, in a few steps, turn right and follow the small road. This is Shoemaker Street (unmarked when I was last here). (See Map 9-4.)

1.1   In a short distance, at the intersection of Shoemaker and Tilden Streets, cross Tilden to Pierce Mill. (See Map 9-4.) When I was last here there were no street signs. (CAUTION: There was also no crosswalk over Tilden when I was last here.)

Pierce Mill was one of several grist mills located on Rock Creek. The mill was built in the 1820s by Isaac Pierce and operated until near the end of the century. It then lay idle until the 1930s, when it was restored as a WPA project. The mill is still in operation today and you can buy some of its processed flour and meal.

1.1   From Pierce Mill, walk up Tilden Street to the west, away from the bridge over Rock Creek.
       (CAUTION: There are no sidewalks along this part of Tilden and the street is sometimes busy with traffic.)

The small stone building a short distance up Tilden Street, in middle of the divided street, is Isaac Pierce's spring house. The structure was built in 1801.

0.9   At the first street intersecting Tilden from the right, turn right. This is Linnean Avenue, but when I was last here there was no street sign.

Up the hill on Linnean Avenue, to your right, are the Hillwood Museum and Grounds. The late socialite Marjorie Merriweather Post used her Post cereal inheritance to build this estate. Her passion was collecting articles from the Russian czarist empire, and her collection, including many Faberge eggs, is now on display. Unfortunately, entrance to the main museum is by appointment only, but you can stroll the grounds between 11:00 am and 3:00 pm without prior arrangement. The grounds include many lovely gardens in different styles as well as several smaller museums. You will be asked for a donation on entering the grounds. Allow yourself at least an hour for a visit.

0.7   At the top of the hill on Linnean Avenue, at its intersection with Upton Street, turn sharply to the left onto Upton.

A short way along Upton Street, the land drops off steeply to your left, and there are a few architecturally interesting houses built into the hillside.

0.2   At the intersection of Upton Street and Connecticut Avenue, turn right onto Connecticut.

The ultramodern glass-faced building across Connecticut Avenue at Upton Street is the headquarters of the Intelsat Corporation.

0.0   Just after crossing Veazey Terrace on Connecticut Avenue, you reach the Van Ness Metro Station and the end of the hike. There are number of places to eat along Connecticut Avenue near the Metro station between Van Ness Street and Windom Place.

NOTES

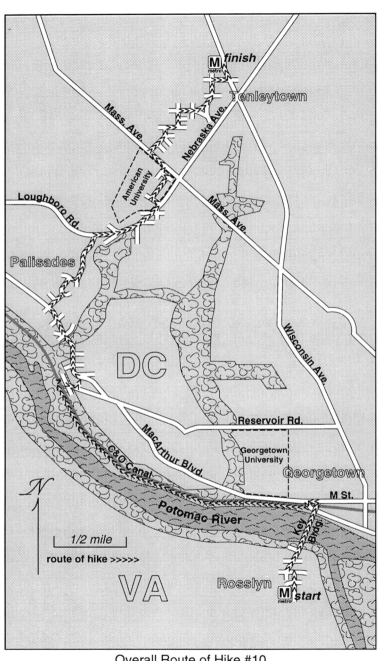

Overall Route of Hike #10
Rosslyn to Tenleytown

HIKE #10

**A mini-highrise city; a long trek up the C&O Canal;
a climb past lovely (sometimes spectacular)
houses; a campus stroll; and a once-disreputable
town turned middle-class in-town suburb.**

From: Rosslyn Metro Station (Virginia)

To: Tenleytown Metro Station (D.C.)

Via: The Rosslyn neighborhood, Key Bridge, the
             C&O Canal, MacArthur Boulevard, the
             Palisades neighborhood, Loughboro Road,
             American University, American University
             Park, and Tenleytown.

Distance: 6.6 miles

Duration: 3 hours 10 minutes if you walk at 2.5 miles per
             hour and make two 15-minute stops.

Highlights

This hike begins amid the modern high-rise buildings of
Rosslyn in Virginia. From here you will cross the Potomac
River to D.C. on Key Bridge and begin a long trek to the west
on the tow path of the rustic Chesapeake and Ohio Canal.
Leaving the canal, you will climb out of the Potomac River
gorge and then walk west along MacArthur Boulevard past
some country cottages and an old farmhouse. Next you will
hike north and uphill through the Palisades neighborhood, past
progressively ritzier houses, and then turn east and follow
Loughboro Road and Nebraska Avenue to American
University. After strolling the campus, you will walk through
the mature in-town suburb of American University Park and
come to Wisconsin Avenue and the end of the hike at the
center of Tenleytown.

Things to Know Before You Start

*All distances shown in parentheses below indicate miles to the
end of the hike.*

Intermediate Metro Stations

None.

Places to Stop for a Rest

Convenient rest stops along the route are: the picnic area along the C&O Canal at Fletcher's Boathouse (3.6 miles) and the campus of American University (1.6 miles).

Places to Stop and Eat

The shopping mall next to the Rosslyn Metro Station (6.6 miles) has a number of places to eat and get carry-out food, including an excellent delicatessen. A refreshment stand is located along the C&O Canal at Fletcher's Boathouse (3.6 miles). Just past Dana Place on MacArthur Boulevard (2.8 miles) are several good, small restaurants. On the American University campus there is a fast food restaurant in the Butler Pavilion (1.3 miles). Finally, at the end of the hike, along Wisconsin Avenue near the Tenleytown Metro station (0.0 miles), are a few restaurants and fast food places .

Public Rest Rooms

Public rest rooms along the route are located at: the shopping mall next to the Rosslyn Metro station (6.6 miles), across the canal from Fletcher's Boathouse (3.6 miles), and in the Butler Pavilion on the American University campus (1.3 miles)

On-Route Directions After You Start

Numbers in the left margin indicate miles to the end of the hike. Unless otherwise indicated, maps are oriented north to top of page.

6.6   When you reach the top of the long escalator at the Rosslyn Metro station, make a U-turn to the left, through the fare card gates, and walk out of the covering building to the street. On reaching the street, turn to the left. You are now following Moore Street north.

        To your right, immediately after passing through the fare gates, is the entrance to a small multi-level shopping mall -- Rosslyn Center. The mall has a number of places to eat and get carry-out food, including an excellent delicatessen. There are also public rest rooms on the second level of the mall.

6.5   After passing under a pedestrian overpass, at the intersection of Moore Street and the eastbound lanes of Lee Highway, turn left (west) onto Lee and walk under another pedestrian overpass. (See Map 10-1.)

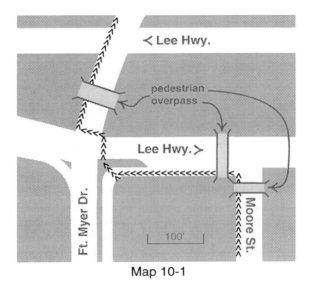

Map 10-1

6.5-   In one short block, at the traffic light, where eastbound Lee Highway intersects Fort Myer Drive, make a half turn to the right and cross an access road to a pedestrian island. From the pedestrian island, cross eastbound Lee Highway. (See Map 10-1.)

On the northeast corner of the intersection of eastbound Lee Highway and Fort Myer Drive is a plaque briefly describing the history of Rosslyn. The recent high-rise development of Rosslyn included an unusual experiment in urban design. The development plan called for pedestrian walkways connecting the second floors of all buildings. The purpose was to create an elevated pedestrian level separated from street-level vehicular traffic. Unfortunately, the plan has never been fully implemented, so the idea remains untested.

6.5-   After crossing eastbound Lee Highway, turn left and
cross Fort Myer Drive. On the other side of Fort
Myer, turn right and follow the drive north under a
third pedestrian overpass and across the westbound
lanes of Lee Highway. (See Map 10-1.)

6.2   Walk onto Francis Scott Key Bridge crossing the
Potomac from Virginia to the District of Columbia.

*The Potomac flows under Key Bridge from left to right.
Its watershed includes the Shenandoah Valley of
Virginia and a large part of Maryland and West
Virginia.   Directly across the bridge in D.C. is
Georgetown, located where it is because this is as far
upriver as colonial settlers could establish a practical
seaport.*

*On a rise above the river on the D.C. side, about forty-
five degrees to your left as you walk across the bridge,
stand the redbrick buildings and stone towers of
Georgetown University. On the riverbank below the
university is the green-and-white home of the
Washington Canoe Club, the oldest such organization
in the U.S. About a hundred yards to the right of the
club on the riverbank lies a stone embankment that
was the entrance to the Aqueduct Bridge, which once
carried canal boats over the Potomac from the
Chesapeake and Ohio Canal on the Washington side
to a canal on the Virginia side that connected Rosslyn
to Alexandria. For a time the Aqueduct Bridge served
both canal boats and, on a superstructure, highway
and rail traffic. The one remaining pier of the bridge
is just visible near the Virginia bank of the river.*

5.9   On the D.C. side of Key Bridge, turn left (west) onto
M Street. (See Map 10-2.)

5.8   In a short distance, at the traffic light where M Street
intersects the Whitehurst Freeway on your left,
follow the sidewalk around to the left along the
Whitehurst Freeway. (See Map 10-2.)

5.8-   In a short distance, where the sidewalk ends after
crossing over the canal, walk down a narrow flight
of steps to your left. At the bottom of these steps
turn left (west) onto the gravel tow path of the canal.

As you walk on the tow path here, the canal should
be to your right. (See Map 10-2.)

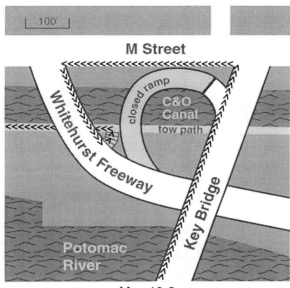

Map 10-2

*The C&O Canal connected the port of Georgetown,
just behind you to the east, to Cumberland, Maryland,
183 miles ahead of you to the west. When the canal
was in operation, the wide stretch you are now walking
along was lined with canal boats, most carrying coal
and waiting to be unloaded. Drawn by mules, the
boats moved at a comfortable walking speed of two
and a half to three miles per hour and usually were
stopped at night to rest the mules and the crew. The
mules were stabled in the bow and the captain and his
family lived in a cabin in the stern. The family acted
as crew, with the children serving as mule drivers. The
canal was declared a national historic park in 1977,
largely through the efforts of Supreme Court Justice
William O. Douglas, an avid tow path hiker.*

*Distance along the C&O Canal from Georgetown to
Cumberland is marked by mileposts just to the left of
the tow path. You will find milepost 2 slightly less than
one mile from where you turned onto the tow path.*

5.3   Continue west on the tow path over two small bridges spanning spillways from the canal to the Potomac.

The wide blacktop path to your left, paralleling the tow path, follows the alignment on the old Georgetown Branch of the Baltimore and Ohio (B&O) railroad. The branch line connected the Georgetown waterfront with the B&O main line in Maryland. The B&O served much of the same market as the canal and was a principal cause of the canal's financial difficulties and its eventual demise. The canal ceased operations in 1924 after the latest of a series of disastrous floods wreaked more damaged than was economically feasible to repair. The rail branch line continued operations for several decades after the canal closed, serving the declining industries along the Georgetown waterfront. Today, the waterfront is prime real estate for residences and offices and the B&O rail right-of-way is being made into the Capital Crescent Trail, which will extend five miles from Georgetown to Silver Spring, Maryland.

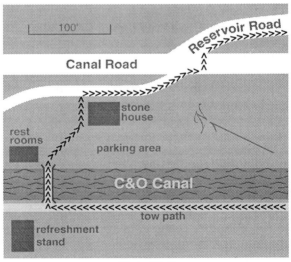

Map 10-3

3.6   About a quarter of a mile past mile post 3 and about a hundred yards past an earthen pathway (with culvert) crossing the canal, turn right and cross over the canal on a wooden footbridge. (See Map 10-3.) To the left before you cross the footbridge are picnic

grounds and a refreshment stand at Fletcher's
Boathouse. On the other side of the footbridge, to
the left, are public rest rooms.

3.6-   After crossing the canal on the footbridge, walk
diagonally to your right across a parking area to a
white stone house and ascend a small set of steps just
to the left of the house. At the top of these steps,
turn right and walk up a paved one-lane access road.
(See Map 10-3.)

(CAUTION: There are no crosswalks or sidewalks
ahead, and you must pass through a busy and
difficult intersection with fast-moving traffic.)

3.6-   In short distance, the one-lane access road merges
into a larger two-lane road. This is Canal Road. On
the other side of Canal Road is Reservoir Road,
which leads uphill and to the right. (When I was last
here there were no signs for either of these roads.)
Cross Canal Road and walk up the right side of
Reservoir Road on a narrow sidewalk.   (See Map
10-3.)

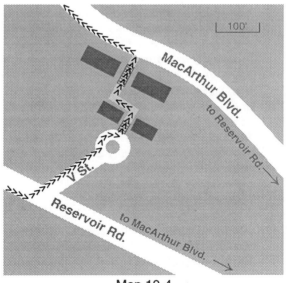

Map 10-4

3.5   After passing an alleyway on your left, at the
intersection of Reservoir Road and V Street, turn left

and walk up V Street. (See Map 10-4.) (CAUTION: There is no crosswalk over Reservoir Road here.)

3.5-   Where V Street ends in a small traffic circle, ascend a short flight of steps at the opposite side of the circle. At the top of these steps, turn left for a few paces, and then turn right and ascend a second flight of steps. At the top of this second set of steps, turn left onto the sidewalk of a major divided city street, MacArthur Boulevard.   (See Map 10-4.)

MacArthur Boulevard, called Conduit Road until 1942, is built on top of an aqueduct carrying the city's drinking water to a filtration plant a few blocks behind you. The aqueduct was cut into the hillside leading up from the Potomac, creating a level strip upon which a road could easily be laid. The hillside neighborhood on both sides of MacArthur Boulevard is known as the Palisades. The area was mostly farmland, with a few scattered summer houses, until very near the end of the 19th century. One story has it that the Palisades developed slowly because competing developers of nearby areas spread rumors that living near the river was unhealthful. In any case, the area was nearly fully built up by the beginning of World War II, with mostly modest houses located low on the hillside and some of the city's grandest mansions sited near its summit. Two houses are worth taking note of as you walk along MacArthur. The first, number 4933, is the large stone house on your right just before a wooded area. Built in the 1890s, the house was first occupied by one of a group of Canadian developers who envisioned the Palisades becoming an expensive Victorian suburb. The second house, number 5066, is the large frame house on your left before you reach Dana Place. Built around 1850, this is one of the neighborhood's original farmhouses.

2.8   After walking some distance, just before reaching a commercial block, at the intersection of MacArthur Boulevard and Dana Place, cross and then turn right onto Dana.

There are restaurants along MacArthur in the first block past Dana, making this a good place to stop for lunch or a snack.

2.7   In two blocks, just before reaching "DO NOT ENTER" signs at the intersection of Dana Place with Eskridge Terrace to the left and University Terrace to the right, turn left onto Eskridge.

2.5   At the next intersection, where Eskridge Terrace ends at Garfield Street, turn right onto Garfield.

2.5-   At the next intersection, where Garfield Street ends at University Terrace, turn left onto University.

2.1   In one long block, where University Terrace ends at its intersection with Loughboro Road, turn right onto Loughboro.

2.0   Where Chain Bridge Road intersects from the right and Indian Lane intersects from the left, continue straight as Loughboro Road becomes Nebraska Avenue.

> *The wooded area to your right, near the end of the first block after the above intersection, was the site of Battery Kemble. This artillery emplacement was one component of an elaborate ring of fortifications created all around Washington during the Civil War. At that time, this was mostly open farmland, miles from the built-up part of the city. The high ground, commanding the surrounding countryside, was an ideal site for a major battery.*

1.7   At the intersection of Nebraska Avenue with Newark Street (on the right) and Rockwood Parkway (on the left), cross to the left side of Nebraska and continue along the avenue in the same direction on the other side.

1.6   In a short distance, turn left through the John M. Reeves Gate onto the campus of the American University. Walk directly away from Nebraska past a parking area on your right. (See Map 10-5.)

1.5   Immediately after passing the first major campus building (the Bender Library) on your right, turn right, leaving the domed McKinley Building on your left. You should now be walking on a wide sidewalk past a row of campus buildings on your left and a small road and grass mall on your right. (See Map 10-5.)

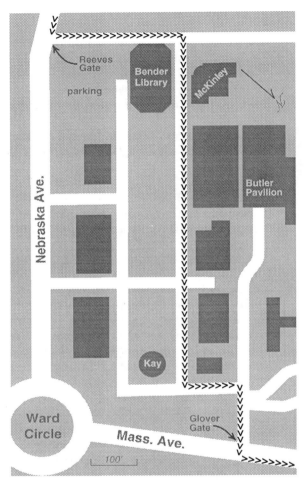

Map 10-5

American University is one of the city's major private universities. It was founded with help from the Methodist Episcopal Church and incorporated by the U.S. Congress in 1893. The university opened classes downtown in the Foggy Bottom neighborhood while the present campus was slowly developed. Progress was delayed when the university donated the present campus site to the U.S. Army to use as part of a testing ground for poison gas during World War I. Classes finally opened on this site in 1920. In nearby Spring Valley, one of Washington's most expensive residential developments, recent excavations uncovered some poison gas munitions that had been buried there since the end of Word War I, unbeknown to the affluent homeowners, some of whom had to be evacuated from their palatial residences for days on end while an army bomb disposal squad cleared the area.

1.3   Where the row of campus buildings on your left ends, just past the round Kay Spiritual Life Center on your right, turn left onto another sidewalk. (See Map 10-5.)

1.3-   In a short distance, at the first intersection, turn right toward a campus gate. (See Map 10-5.) (NOTE: One block in the opposite direction from the gate, are public rest rooms, a convenience store, and a fast food restaurant in the Butler Pavilion.)

1.2   In a short distance, exit the campus through the Glover Gate and, at the traffic light and crosswalk, walk straight across (the unmarked) Massachusetts Avenue. After crossing, turn left and walk along the right side of the avenue. (See Map 10-5.)

1.1   Where 45th Street intersects Massachusetts Avenue, cross and then turn right onto 45th.

Within view, a short distance past 45th on the left side of Massachusetts, is a statue of John Wesley (1703-1791), the founder of Methodism. Although it is unusual to see a theologian memorialized astride a horse, churchmen riding horseback must have been a common sight in Wesley's day.

0.9   Where 45th Street ends at its intersection with Van Ness Street, turn right onto Van Ness.

0.8   In one block, where 44th Street intersects Van Ness Street from the left, turn left (north) onto 44th.

0.6   In two blocks, at the intersection of 44th and Warren Streets, turn right (east) onto Warren.

0.5   After crossing 43rd Street on Warren Street, where the road branches to the right and left, follow the left (northeast) branch.

0.4   At the first four-way intersection (42nd and Yuma
       Streets) continue slightly to the left of straight
       (north) onto 42nd.

0.3   In one block, at the intersection of 42nd and
       Albemarle Streets, turn right (east) onto Albemarle.

0.1   In one block, at the intersection of Albemarle Street
       and Wisconsin Avenue, turn left (north) onto
       Wisconsin.

0.0   In the middle of the first block on Wisconsin
       Avenue, you come to an entrance to the Tenleytown
       Metro Station and the end of the hike.

       There are several restaurants in the first few blocks
       of Wisconsin north of Albemarle.

       The next intersection, where River Road branches off
       Wisconsin Avenue, is the center of the old community
       of Tenleytown.   Wisconsin Avenue was a major
       commercial   route   beginning   well   before   the
       Revolutionary War, connecting the tobacco farms in
       Maryland with the port of Georgetown.   River Road
       was built in 1779. A few years later, a man by the
       name of John Tennally built a tavern at the
       intersection and began the slow development of the site
       as a country village. A new and larger tavern, called
       the Tennallytown Inn, was built in the 1850s and
       survived until 1939. Tenleytown is the highest point in
       the city (note the communications towers here today),
       a fact that made it of strategic importance to the
       defense of Washington during the Civil War.   The
       largest of the fortifications surrounding the city, Fort
       Reno, was built here, a short distance east of
       Wisconsin Avenue. At the end of the war, the land on
       which Fort Reno stood was subdivided into small lots,
       many of which were sold to recently freed slaves. By
       the early 20th century, Tennallytown had grown into a
       distinct, racially mixed, working-class community.
       However, the community had gained an unsavory
       reputation from the rowdiness and gambling
       associated with its taverns, and it was considered by
       the city's dominant powers to be standing in the way of
       progress.   With improvements in transportation,
       middle-class Washingtonians began spreading into the
       area and did not like what they saw in Tenleytown,

particularly the black community on the site of Fort Reno. To deal with "the problem," a so-called civic improvement scheme was devised under which the properties on the site were condemned for the purpose of building schools and a park.   The resulting development is pretty much what you see around you today.   Incidentally, the name of the community -- which had been variously spelled and pronounced through its history -- was officially established as Tenleytown by the city post office in 1920.

NOTES

_____

_____

_____

_____

_____

_____

_____

_____

_____

_____

_____

_____

_____

_____

_____

_____

_____

_____

_____

_____

_____

_____

_____

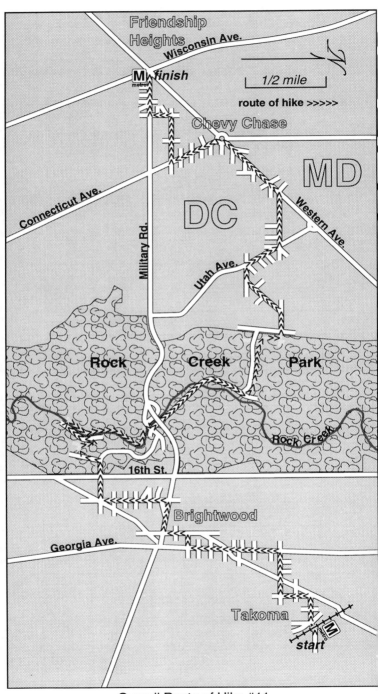

Overall Route of Hike #11
Takoma to Friendship Heights

HIKE #11

**A community that beat city hall; the city's only
Civil War battle and its heroes; a stroll along a
babbling brook; and an old new-town.**

From: Takoma Metro Station (D.C.)

To: Friendship Heights Metro Station (D.C.-
                 Maryland)

Via: The Takoma neighborhood (D.C.), Georgia
                 Avenue, Fort Stevens, Brightwood and
                 Brightwood Park, Rock Creek Park, and the
                 Chevy Chase neighborhood (D.C.).

Distance: 7.6 miles

Duration: 3 hours 45 minutes if you walk at 2.5 miles per
                 hour and make three 15-minute stops.

Highlights

This hike begins by meandering west through the old intown
D.C. suburb of Takoma past some fine turn-of-the-century
mansions. You will then turn south and hike down Georgia
Avenue, past a small cemetery where Civil War soldiers are
buried, to Fort Stevens, where the soldiers were killed in the
only Civil War battle fought within the District of Columbia.
From Fort Stevens you will go west on Military Road and then
south on 14th Street through the old Brightwood Park
subdivision. Next you will walk west and descend steeply into
the densely wooded valley of Rock Creek Park. At the bottom
of the valley, you will follow Rock Creek as it flows, in a near
wilderness, around the stones and boulders for which it is
named. Continuing north, along less-wild stretches of the
creek, you will eventually climb out of the valley near
Bingham Drive. You will now walk generally west, through
mature in-town suburbs, to the center of the turn-of-the-
century planned community of Chevy Chase. After hiking
through Chevy Chase, you will come to Wisconsin Avenue
and the end of the hike at Friendship Heights.

Things to Know Before You Start

All distances shown in parentheses below indicate miles to the end of the hike.

Intermediate Metro Stations

None.

Places to Stop for a Rest

Convenient rest stops along the route are: Fort Stevens (6.3 miles), the picnic grounds near the Fitzgerald Tennis Stadium (5.1 miles), the wild stretch along Rock Creek where creek-side boulders make wonderful seats (4.7 to 4.0 miles), and the picnic grounds along Rock Creek (3.8 miles).

Places to Stop and Eat

Many mostly neighborhood-oriented restaurants lie along the route in the two blocks of Connecticut Avenue south of Chevy Chase Circle (1.1-). Even more, of greater variety, are available at the end of the hike in Friendship Heights (0.0 miles). The hike offers three places to picnic: two formal picnic grounds in Rock Creek Park (5.1 and 3.8 miles) and the wild stretch along Rock Creek (4.7 to 4.0 miles). Note, however, that in good weather, formal picnic sites in the park are likely to be occupied.

Public Rest Rooms

Public rest rooms are located at: the picnic grounds near the Fitzgerald Tennis Stadium (5.1 miles) and the picnic grounds along Rock Creek (3.8 miles).

Some Cautions

Part of the route of this hike follows dirt trails in Rock Creek Park that may be muddy and slippery. One trail is unmarked and may be difficult to follow, particularly in autumn when it is covered with newly fallen leaves.

On-Route Directions After You Start

Numbers in the left margin indicate miles to the end of the hike. Unless otherwise indicated, maps are oriented north to top of page.

7.6   Immediately on leaving the Takoma Metro station (there is only one exit), make a U-turn to the right and walk under the rail bridge along Cedar Street (unmarked). Continue on Cedar through its intersection with Blair Road and 4th Street. This complicated intersection is not well marked. (See Map 11-1.)

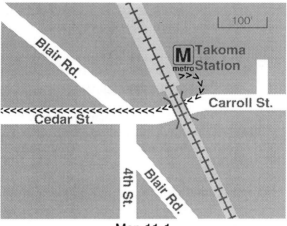

Map 11-1

For the first few blocks, this hike threads its way through the historic D.C. neighborhood of Takoma. Many of the houses along Cedar Street were built in the early 20th century and reflect the Victorian character of the neighborhood's origins. Together with the adjacent town of Takoma Park, Maryland, D.C.'s Takoma began in the 1880s as a commuter suburb connected to downtown Washington by passenger service on the B&O (now CSX) Railroad. The Metro tracks are built within the CSX railroad right-of-way. The old railroad passenger station was located just south of the present Takoma Metro station. Today, though surrounded by a sprawling city and suburbs, the community retains much of the peaceful, small-town character of its beginnings. In recent decades, however, the peace of the community was threatened by transportation planners and real estate speculators. In the early 1960s a ten-lane freeway was proposed that would have bisected, and destroyed, the community. Fighting the powerful "highway lobby," the community organized and, against all odds, killed the freeway. Not coincidentally, this was the end to all major freeway development in the city. At about the same time, as African Americans began moving into the previously all-white neighborhood, some unscrupulous real estate speculators worked to panic white home owners into moving out and selling cheap. To counter this threat, Takoma joined with several adjacent city neighborhoods in forming Neighbors, Inc. -- an organization promoting the orderly integration of the area. As a result of these efforts, Takoma is now stable, middle-class, and fully integrated.

7.4   In two blocks, at the intersection of Cedar and 6th Streets, turn left (south) onto 6th.

7.2   Two blocks after turning onto 6th Street, at the intersection of 6th and Aspen Streets, turn right (west) onto Aspen.

7.1   One block after turning onto Aspen Street, cross Piney Branch Road and continue west on Aspen.

6.9   At the intersection of Aspen Street and Georgia Avenue, turn left (south) onto Georgia. Stay on the left (east) side of Georgia.

Today's Georgia Avenue, with its densely packed small businesses, is the descendent of the 19th-century 7th Street Turnpike -- a major commercial toll road connecting the early capital city downtown to farms in the outlying regions of D.C. and neighboring Maryland. The avenue is an extension of 7th Street, downtown, one of the original commercial streets of the city. In the 19th century the sparsely settled farming community surrounding the 7th Street Turnpike was known as Brightwood. The name today refers to a smaller area generally to the west of Georgia Avenue. The avenue received its present name largely through the efforts of citizens attempting to gain support for local improvements from an influential senator from Georgia. Unfortunately, the senator died a short time after the renaming.

On the left (east) side of Georgia Avenue, between Whittier and Van Buren Streets, lies a small Federal cemetery containing the graves of forty Union soldiers killed at the battle of Fort Stevens (described below). As you walk south down Georgia Avenue you will be advancing on Fort Stevens along the same route taken by a Confederate Army force in 1864.

6.3   At the intersection of Georgia Avenue and Quackenbos Street, turn right (west) onto Quackenbos.

Before reaching 13th Street (in one block), Quackenbos passes the reconstructed Fort Stevens on your right. Fort Stevens was built in 1861, as part of a ring of forts and artillery batteries emplaced all around Washington, and was located specifically to guard the approach to the Capital from the north along the 7th Street Turnpike. The fort was built on the property of an African American dairy-woman, Betty Thomas, whose house was leveled so its basement could be used for ammunition storage. On July 11 and 12, 1864, the importance of Fort Stevens was proven in battle. A Confederate force under General Jubal A. Early was blocked at the fort from advancing down the turnpike and threatening the city. This was the only Civil War battle fought in the District of Columbia. President Lincoln witnessed the battle from within the fort and exposed himself to enemy fire. This incident led to many, probably apocryphal, stories. In one such, Oliver Wendell Holmes, Jr. -- then a captain in the 6th Massachusetts Regiment stationed at the fort and later a famous justice of the U.S. Supreme Court -- shouted to the tall, unrecognized figure, "Get down, you damn fool, before you get shot!" It is also reported that Lincoln personally consoled Betty Thomas for the loss of her home, but there is no record of her receiving any financial compensation from the government.

6.2   At the intersection of Quackenbos and 13th Streets, turn left (south) onto 13th.

6.1   In one block, at the intersection of 13th Street and
        Military Road turn right (west) onto Military.

        *Military Road was built originally by the Union Army
        to connect the tier of Civil War fortifications, including
        Fort Stevens, that protected the city from the north. To
        appreciate the importance of these fortifications, it
        must be remembered that Confederate General Robert
        E. Lee twice took his Army of Northern Virginia across
        the Potomac north of Washington -- once before the
        Battle of Antietam and again before the Battle of
        Gettysburg. If he had won either of these battles, he
        could have encircled the city.*

5.9   At the intersection of Military Road and 14th Street,
        turn left (south) onto 14th.

        *Between here and the next turn at Kennedy Street, the
        hike passes through the late 19th- and early 20th-
        century subdivision of Brightwood Park.*

5.4   One block past Longfellow Street, at the intersection
        of 14th Street, Colorado Avenue, and Kennedy
        Street, turn right (west) onto Kennedy. (NOTE: The
        last time I was here, the sign for Kennedy Street was
        hidden behind a traffic light.)

5.3   At the intersection of Kennedy and 16th Streets,
        cross 16th and continue in the same direction (west)
        on Morrow Drive. Use the blacktop path along the
        left (south) side of Morrow.

5.2   Follow the blacktop path as it turns left (south) away
        from Morrow Drive along an unnamed road leading
        to the Fitzgerald Tennis Stadium. There is a baseball
        backstop at this turn along with a sign pointing to
        Carter Barron Amphitheater Fringe Parking. (See
        Map 11-2.)

5.1   Just before reaching the tennis stadium, turn right
        and cross the road toward a playground and public
        rest rooms at the edge of the woods of Rock Creek
        Park. (See Map 11-2.)

5.1-   At the back of the playground, where the woods
        begin, midway between two stone fireplaces, enter

the woods on an unmarked but well-used dirt trail.
(See Map 11-2.)

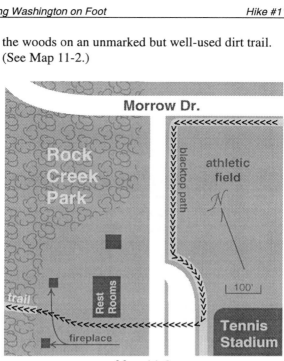

·Map 11-2

5.0   In a short distance, follow the trail as it turns to the
       right around a large bolder. (See Map 11-3.)

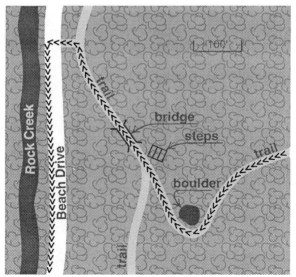

Map 11-3

5.0-   A short distance downhill, pass some dilapidated
       wooden steps on your right and walk across a short
       wooden bridge. (CAUTION: Do not use the steps,
       and be careful of the condition of the bridge.) (See
       Map 11-3.)

4.9   At the bottom of the hill (before the trail starts
       uphill), there is a two-lane blacktop road to your left.
       This is Beach Drive. At this point, leave the trail and
       cross Beach Drive. After crossing Beach Drive, turn
       left and walk south along its right side. As you walk
       here, Rock Creek should be on your right, flowing in
       the same direction you are walking. (See Map 11-3.)

       *Rock Creek Park was established in 1890 with strong
       support from the developers of Chevy Chase (see
       below). The Park consists of 2,100 acres of stream
       valley cut by the waters of Rock Creek and intersecting
       the boundary between the upland Piedmont geological
       zone, sloping gradually up to the Appalachian
       Mountains to the west and north, and the Coastal
       Plain, sloping down to the Atlantic Ocean and the
       Chesapeake Bay to the east and south. At the creek's
       southern end, the C&O Canal joins it just before it
       empties into the Potomac River between Foggy Bottom
       and Georgetown. Much of the park consists of a
       mature hardwood forest that includes oak, ash, beech,
       birch, dogwood, redbud, azalea, and mountain laurel.
       The creek itself, though polluted, contains crayfish and
       several species of swimming fish. On land and among
       the surrounding trees are squirrels, raccoons, and a
       variety of birds, including pileated woodpeckers.
       According to recent reports, there is also a growing
       population of deer and foxes -- right in the heart of the
       city.*

4.7   Where a footbridge crosses over Rock Creek, turn
       right and cross on the bridge.

4.7-   At the far side of the bridge, turn right onto the dirt
       bridle path. As you walk here, Rock Creek should
       again be on your right but it should now be flowing
       opposite to the direction you are walking.

       (NOTE: The creekside here is a great place to take a
       break and enjoy the surroundings. Have a picnic, if
       you brought the makings.)

4.0   Where the bridle path leaves the woods and turns to
        the left along the side of a paved, two-lane road,
        leave the trail and cross the road. (See Map 11-4.)

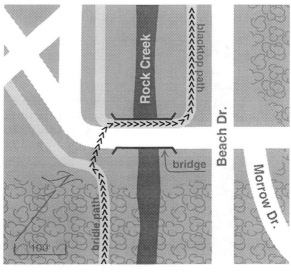

Map 11-4

4.0-   On the opposite side of the road, you will find a
        blacktop path paralleling the road. Turn right onto
        this path and follow it and the road over Rock Creek
        on a balustrade-sided concrete bridge. (See Map
        11-4.)

4.0-   On the far side of the bridge, follow the blacktop
        path to the left alongside Beach Drive. As you walk
        here, Beach Drive should be to your right. Rock
        Creek should now be on your left, flowing opposite
        to the direction you are walking. (See Map 11-4.)

3.9   Walk under the bridge that carries Military Road
        overhead.

        To the left about half a mile, on a hilltop now deep in
        the woods, are the barely discernable ruins of Fort
        DeRussey, another Civil War fortification served by
        Military Road.

3.8   You come to a picnic area with tables, some limited
        shelter, a drinking fountain, and (across Beach
        Drive) public rest rooms.

> *The small cabin at the north end of the picnic ground is of authentic log construction. In the 19th century it stood along 16th Street, occupied by Joaquin Miller, the "Poet of the Sierras." Miller is probably best known for his 1871 poem, "Songs of the Sierras."*

3.5   Follow the blacktop path and Beach Drive across Rock Creek.

3.2   Immediately after the blacktop path crosses Bingham Drive (which intersects Beach Drive from the left), turn left and follow the blacktop path along the right side of Bingham Drive. (See Map 11-5.)

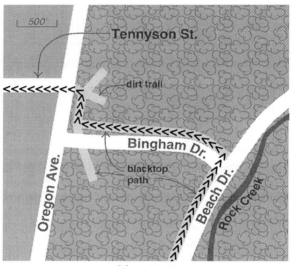

Map 11-5

2.8   Where you intersect another blacktop path from the left, continue along the path you are on, around to the right, away from Bingham Drive. The path now proceeds north along the western edge of Rock Creek Park. You should be able to see Oregon Avenue through the trees to the left, paralleling the path. (See Map 11-5.)

2.7   Just after the path turns diagonally to the right away from Oregon Avenue, a well-used but unmarked dirt trail crosses the blacktop path. Turn left onto the dirt trail and continue west, across Oregon Avenue, and down the left (south) side of Tennyson Street. (See Map 11-5.) (NOTE: The street sign for Tennyson Street is on a telephone pole a short way north of

Tennyson on Oregon Avenue.) (CAUTION: There is no crosswalk at this intersection.)

2.5   At the intersection of Tennyson and 29th Streets, turn half left (southwest) onto 29th.

2.2   At the intersection of 29th and Rittenhouse Streets, turn half right (west) onto Rittenhouse.

2.1   At the intersection of Rittenhouse Street, 30th Street, and Utah Avenue, turn half right (northwest) onto Utah.

1.9   At the intersection of Utah Avenue and Tennyson Street, turn half left (west) onto Tennyson.

1.6   At the intersection of Tennyson Street and Western Avenue, turn half left (southwest) onto Western. (NOTE: Western Avenue forms the boundary between D.C. and Maryland. As you walk along Western Avenue, D.C. is to your left and Maryland is to your right.)

1.1   At the intersection of Western Avenue and Chevy Chase Circle, turn left and walk around the circle (clockwise).

Chevy Chase Circle is the center of the planned community of Chevy Chase. Development of the community was initiated in 1890 as a single, large, private real estate enterprise. One of its original (and grander) homes, built by one of the community's founders, stands on the right (northwest) side of Western Avenue where it intersects the circle. Like Takoma Park, Chevy Chase began as a commuter suburb based on a new transportation. In this case, the new transportation was the extension of Connecticut Avenue from downtown D.C. into Maryland and the construction of an electric streetcar line. Unlike that of Takoma Park, however, the new road and streetcar line were designed and financed privately by Chevy Chase's wealthy developers. Although the houses here are architecturally diverse, the overall plan of Chevy Chase was carefully laid out, and commercial development was restricted to a few locations, one being the west side of Connecticut

Avenue just below the circle. The unusual name, Chevy Chase, was the name of an earlier estate in the area, and refers to a battle that took place in 1388 over a hunting ground or "chase" in the Cheviot Hills on the border separating England and Scotland. Knowledge of the battle was kept alive in popular tales, most recently in Sir Walter Scott's "The Ballad of Chevy Chase." As is the case of Takoma Park, the Maryland part of today's Chevy Chase is an incorporated city, while the D.C. part is a Washington neighborhood.

1.1-   About one-third of the way around the circle, where Connecticut Avenue intersects the circle, turn left (southeast) onto Connecticut.

       There are a number of restaurants in the next two blocks along the right (west) side of Connecticut.

0.7   At the intersection of Connecticut Avenue and Livingston Street, turn right (west) onto Livingston.

0.4   At the intersection of 41st and Livingston Streets, cross and then turn left (south) onto 41st.

0.3   At the intersection of 41st Street and Military Road, turn right (west) onto Miliary.

0.0   Where Military Road ends, at its intersection with Western Avenue (when I was last here there was no street sign for Western), turn left and go southwest onto Western Avenue. In a few steps, at the intersection of Western and Wisconsin Avenues, is the entrance to the Chevy Chase Pavilion building and the end of the hike. An entrance to the Friendship Heights Metro station can be found on the lower level of this building, along with several places to eat and public rest rooms. There are also several restaurants to the left (south) down Wisconsin Avenue.

       Diagonally across the intersection of Wisconsin and Western Avenues you can see one of the many stone markers placed in 1791 to delineate the boundary of the District of Columbia. If you want, you can reach the stone marker by crossing under the intersection through the Metro station entrance tunnels.

NOTES

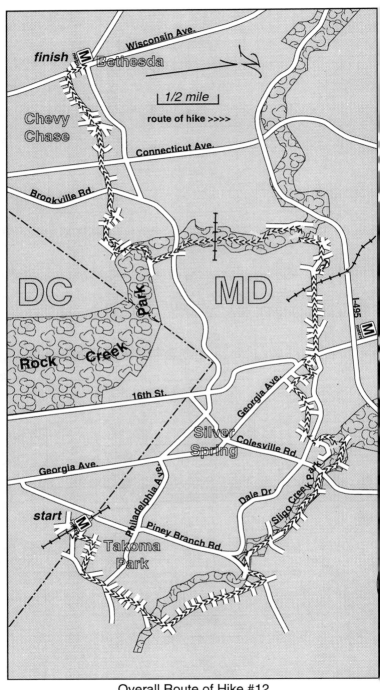

Overall Route of Hike #12
Takoma to Bethesda

HIKE #12

Victorian splendor; a multi-cultural suburb; a long walk up a wooded suburban stream; a women's college in fantasy land; a long walk down a wooded suburban stream; and ascents through the hills of an old and affluent suburb.

From: Takoma Metro Station (D.C.)

To: Bethesda Metro Station (Maryland)

Via: Takoma Park, Sligo Creek Park, Woodside Park, Forest Glen, the Walter Reed Army Medical Center annex, the National Park Seminary, Rock Creek Regional Park, Chevy Chase (Maryland), and Bethesda.

Distance: 10.4 miles

Duration: 5 hours 30 minutes if you walk at 2.5 miles per hour, make five 10-minute stops, and take 30 minutes for lunch.

Highlights

From the Takoma Metro station, the hike takes you through a historic section of Takoma Park, Maryland, along shaded streets and past some exquisite Victorian houses. Still in Takoma Park, you will next walk through a neighborhood of smaller suburban houses that is home to a multi-ethnic mixture of recent immigrants. The hike now descends into the narrow, wooded valley of Sligo Creek Park. Here you will follow the creek past playgrounds and picnic sites and then emerge from the park into a modern suburban development. Soon you will come to the beautiful, quiet, shaded, older development of Woodside Park. Leaving this serene scene, you will walk north a short distance along busy Georgia Avenue and then turn west, following Seminary Road and Linden Lane through quiet suburbs to the Forest Glen Section of Walter Reed Hospital and the decaying architectural fantasy land that is the former National Park Seminary. From here you will hike a short distance through a secluded, almost secret older neighborhood and then plunge steeply into the woods of Rock Creek Regional Park. You will now follow Rock Creek south, under a trestle of the abandoned Georgetown Branch of the B&O Railroad, past athletic fields and horse paddocks, to Meadowbrook Park. Here you will cross Rock Creek and climb out of the stream valley through ritzy suburbs and then hike through the historic community of Chevy Chase, Maryland. Finally, you will emerge onto busy Wisconsin Avenue, in the commercial heart of Bethesda, and reach the end of the hike at the Bethesda Metro station.

Things to Know Before You Start

All distances shown in parentheses below indicate miles to the end of the hike.

Intermediate Metro Stations

The Forest Glen Metro station is about half of a mile north of the intersection of Georgia Avenue and Seminary Road (5.1 miles).

Places to Stop for a Rest

Convenient rest stops along the route are: Sligo Creek Park (8.0 to 6.4 miles) and Meadowbrook Park (2.1 miles).

Places to Stop and Eat

A number of small ethnic restaurants are located at the intersection of Flower Avenue and Piney Branch Road (8.2 miles). Just before reaching Seminary Road on Georgia Avenue (5.2 miles) is a good sit-down delicatessen. Finally, many and varied restaurants are available near the end of the hike in Bethesda, including the multi-shop Food Court next to the Metro station. If you bring your own food, there are a number of good picnic sites in Sligo Creek Park (8.0 to 6.4 miles).

Public Rest Rooms

Public rest rooms are located at: Meadowbrook Park (2.1 miles) and the Food Court at the end of the hike (0.0 miles).

Some Cautions

This is a long hike and you may want to consider taking two
days, hiking from the Takoma Metro station to the Forest Glen
Metro station on the first day and from the Forest Glen Metro
station to the Bethesda Metro station on the second day.

For a short distance, this hike descends steeply through woods
on an unmarked dirt trail that can be slippery and treacherous.
It may also be difficult to follow, particularly in autumn when
it is covered with newly fallen leaves.

On-Route Directions After You Start

*Numbers in the left margin indicate miles to the end of the
hike. Unless otherwise indicated, maps are oriented north to
top of page.*

10.4 There is only one exit from the Takoma Metro
   station. On exiting, walk straight away from the
   station along the left side of a street that is to your
   right. This is Carroll Street. (See Map 12-1.)
   Continue on Carroll across a Metro access road to
   your left.

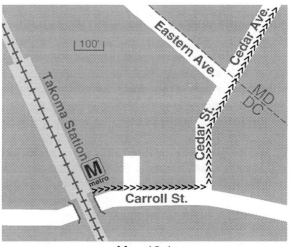

Map 12-1

10.4- In a short distance, at the intersection of Carroll and
   Cedar Streets, cross and then turn left onto Cedar.
   (See Map 12-1.)

10.3   Continue straight on Cedar Street past its intersection
        with Eastern Avenue to your left. (See Map 12-1.)
        At this point Cedar Street becomes Cedar Avenue as
        you leave the District of Columbia and enter the
        small, historic city of Takoma Park, Maryland.

*Takoma Park -- together with the adjacent D.C.
neighborhood of Takoma -- began in 1883 as a
speculative real estate venture of Benjamin Franklin
Gilbert. Gilbert's basic idea was to offer affordable
housing in a small-town environment to the rapidly
increasing numbers of Federal civil servants. Recently
inaugurated railroad passenger service to downtown
Washington offered the means by which government
employees could live in Gilbert's cooler, quieter, more
healthful suburb and still work in the crowded city.
The low purchase price of most of the houses (between
$1,000 and $5,000) made home ownership practical
for workers with modest incomes. The community was
not wholly for those of limited means, however. Many
one-of-a-kind, architect-designed, Victorian mansions
are scattered through the older parts of the city.
Gilbert's enthusiasm for Takoma Park led him to
overextend himself in building a large resort hotel.
This, plus the nationwide financial crisis of 1893, led
to his gradual financial downfall. The town, however,
continued to expand through the early 20th century.
Many of the houses erected during this period were
purchased out of the Sears, Roebuck catalog, and the
precut lumber and other building materials were
delivered on the same railroad line that carried
commuters to and from downtown. The fortunes of
Takoma Park's residents declined during the Great
Depression, and the housing shortage during World
War II led to many of the large houses being
subdivided into apartments. In recent years, however,
the surviving small-town character of the community
has attracted affluent home buyers, and most of the
large houses have been restored to their original
Victorian splendor. The older sections of both Takoma
Park and Takoma are included in the National
Register of Historic Places. Another part of the
character of Takoma Park is the existence of a sort of
good-natured, 1960s-style counterculture, manifested
in health food shops, alternative bookstores, and an
official ordinance declaring the city a nuclear-free
zone.*

10.2　In one block, at the intersection of Cedar and Tulip Avenues, turn right onto Tulip.

The large house on your right as you turn the corner from Cedar to Tulip Avenue is known as the Thomas-Siegler House. Built in 1884, it was the first house completed in Takoma Park. The original owner, Horace Thomas, was the town's first postmaster and first railroad stationmaster. As part of an effort to preserve the site, the rear part of the property, including a large carriage house, has been purchased by the city and converted to a park.

9.9　In three blocks, at the intersection of Tulip and Carroll Avenues, turn left onto Carroll.

The small Tudor-revival service station at the intersection of Tulip and Carroll Avenues was built in 1933 and is one of Takoma Park's interesting fixtures.

9.7　One block after passing a fire house on your right and immediately after crossing Grant Avenue on your left, continue on Carroll as it makes a half turn to the left. The road straight ahead is Ethan Allen Avenue. (See Map 12-2.) (NOTE: When I last passed here, there were no street signs at this intersection.)

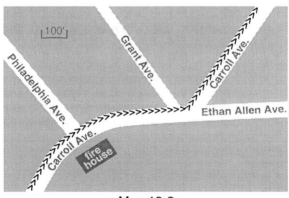

Map 12-2

9.3　Where Jefferson Avenue intersects Carroll Avenue from the left, continue straight on Carroll as Old Carroll Avenue branches off to the right.

9.2   In a short distance, follow Carroll Avenue onto a
         bridge over the wooded Sligo Creek Park.

         *A typical promotional attraction of many early suburbs
         was amusement parks, and Takoma Park was no
         exception. To your right, a short distance down Sligo
         Creek, was the Wildwood amusement park, with hotel
         accommodations, gambling, dancing, and boating on
         a dammed-up section of the creek. The amusement
         park opened in 1900 and was served by its own street
         car line. Because of frequent flash flooding and
         financial problems, Wildwood closed after just a few
         years.*

9.1   A short distance after leaving the bridge over Sligo
         Creek Park, at the traffic light where Carroll Avenue
         intersects Flower Avenue, turn left onto Flower
         Avenue.

         *Immediately after turning onto Flower Avenue you are
         walking through the small campus of Columbia Union
         College. The college and the adjacent Washington
         Adventist Hospital are part of a Seventh Day Adventist
         community located in Takoma Park. In 1903 Gilbert
         persuaded the Seventh Day Adventists to move their
         headquarters to Takoma Park. The Adventists bought
         land and built their General Conference headquarters
         building in the center of the town a few blocks from the
         present Takoma Metro station. Construction of the
         hospital and college followed soon after on this site
         overlooking Sligo Creek.*

         *Farther along Flower Avenue, you enter a multiracial,
         multiethnic, modest-income neighborhood with a large
         population of immigrants from the Caribbean, Latin
         America, and east Asia. One of the many contributions
         of these immigrants is the variety of good and
         inexpensive restaurants centered on the intersection of
         Flower Avenue and Piney Branch Road.*

8.2   At the traffic-light-controlled intersection of Flower
         Avenue and Piney Branch Road, cross and then turn
         left onto Piney Branch.

8.0   At the traffic-light-controlled intersection of Piney
         Branch Road and Sligo Creek Parkway, cross and
         then turn right onto the parkway. In a few steps,

follow a blacktop path that begins on the left side of the parkway. As you walk here, Sligo Creek is to your left.

The narrow, six-and-a-half-mile-long Sligo Creek Park is one of several stream valley parks in Montgomery County, Maryland. These parks were established during the 1930s and represent an amazing feat of foresight and conservation, in light of the intensive development that has occurred in the county in the years since. They also represent an amazing level of cooperation among different interests. Much of the land for Sligo Creek Park was donated by a major land owner, E. Brook Lee, and by adjacent property owners. The rest was acquired by the county with assistance from the federal government.

7.9   In a short distance, after passing a small parking area on the left, follow the path away from the parkway onto a footbridge over Sligo Creek. On the other side of the bridge, follow the blacktop path to the right. Sligo Creek should now be to your right. Continue on the path that follows the creek, keeping to the right past a playground and a grassy area.

7.8   At the far end of the grassy area, follow the path to the right across another footbridge back over Sligo Creek. On the other side of the bridge, follow the path as it turns to the left. The creek should now be on your left and the parkway on your right.

7.6   At the traffic light where Sligo Creek Parkway intersects Wayne Avenue, cross and turn left onto Wayne Avenue, and then follow Wayne onto a bridge over Sligo Creek. (See Map 12-3.)

7.6-   A short distance up Wayne Avenue, turn right onto the blacktop path leading back into Sligo Creek Park. (See Map 12-3.)

7.6-   In a short distance, after passing a playground to your right, continue straight past the intersection with a blacktop path that turns to the right and crosses Sligo Creek. As you walk here, Sligo Creek should be to your right and the Blair High School athletic field to your left. (See Map 12-3.)

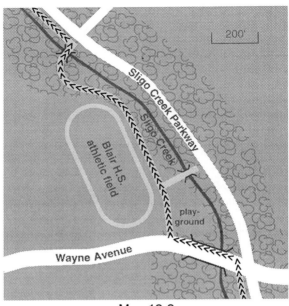

Map 12-3

7.4   After passing the athletic field, follow the path as it
       turns to the right onto another foot-bridge over Sligo
       Creek. On the other side of the bridge, turn to the
       left onto a blacktop path. Sligo Creek should now be
       to your left and Sligo Creek Parkway should be to
       your right. (See Map 12-3.)

7.2   After passing a small parking area to your left,
       continue straight on the path onto a bridge over a
       tributary of Sligo Creek. After crossing this bridge,
       Sligo Creek should still be to your left.

7.0   Continue straight on the blacktop path past a bridge
       over Sligo Creek to your left.

6.8   At the traffic-light-controlled intersection where
       Sligo Creek Parkway crosses Colesville Road, cross
       Colesville and, on the other side, continue straight on
       the blacktop path along the left side of Sligo Creek
       Parkway. Sligo Creek should still be on your left.

6.7   Immediately after passing a foot bridge to your left
       over Sligo Creek, continue straight across a bridge
       over another tributary of the creek.

6.5   At the next foot bridge over Sligo Creek, turn left,
       cross the creek on that bridge, and follow the
       blacktop path to the left on the other side. (See Map
       12-4.)

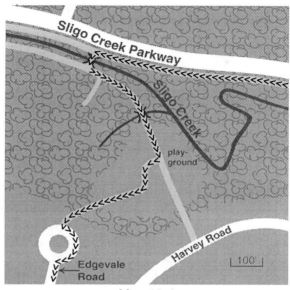

Map 12-4

6.5-   In a few steps, continue straight past a smaller
       blacktop path to your right. (See Map 12-4.)

6.5-   In a short distance, follow the path over a foot bridge
       crossing yet another of tributary to Sligo Creek.
       (See Map 12-4.)

6.4   In a short distance, where there is a playground to
       your left, turn right onto an intersecting blacktop
       path. (See Map 12-4.)

6.3   In a short distance, leave the woods of Sligo Creek
       Park and proceed onto a small traffic circle at the
       end of a street. This is Edgevale Road. Follow
       Edgevale away from the park. (See Map 12-4.)

6.2   At the next intersection, where Edgevale Road meets
       Harvey Road, turn right onto Harvey.

6.1   At the next intersection, where Harvey Road ends at
       Dale Drive, cross and then turn right onto Dale.

(CAUTION: Dale Drive is a busy street, and there is neither a crosswalk nor sidewalks.)

6.1-   In a short distance, at the bottom of the hill on Dale Drive, turn left onto a blacktop footpath passing through a narrow wooded park.

6.0   Where the path ends, at the intersection of Highland Drive and Alton Parkway, turn right from the path onto Highland.

For the next few blocks you will be walking through the lovely old suburban development of Woodside Park. The 182-acre community was laid out in 1923, and most of the houses were built in 1925 and 1926. In order to produce a suitably refined neighborhood, the developer placed certain restrictions on design and construction, among which was the requirement that the cost of building a house had to be at least $6,000.

5.6   At the fifth intersection, where Highland Drive intersects Woodland Drive, turn right onto Woodland. (See Map 12-5.) (NOTE: When I was last here there was no street sign at this intersection. Woodland Drive is the street just past the house at 1437 Highland Drive. If you reach Georgia Avenue, you have gone one block too far.)

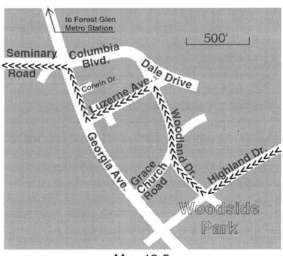

Map 12-5

5.5   At the intersection of Woodland Drive and Grace
        Church Road, turn right and then, after a few steps,
        where the road ahead branches, follow the branch to
        the left back onto Woodland (also unmarked when I
        was last here). (See Map 12-5.)

5.4   At the next intersection, where Woodland Drive
        crosses Luzerne Avenue (before reaching Dale
        Drive), turn left onto Luzerne. (See Map 12-5.)

5.2   At the intersection of Luzerne Avenue and Georgia
        Avenue, turn right (north) onto Georgia. (See Map
        12-5.)

        After crossing Corwin Drive on Georgia Avenue,
        there is a good sit-down delicatessen to your right.
        This is roughly half way through the hike and good
        place to stop for lunch or get some carry-out. Also,
        if you want to discontinue the hike here, proceed in
        the same direction (north) on Georgia Avenue for
        half a mile to the Forest Glen Metro station.

5.1   At the traffic light where Georgia Avenue intersects
        Columbia Boulevard to the right and Seminary Road
        to the left, turn left (west) and walk along the left
        side of Seminary. (See Map 12-5.)

4.9   At the traffic light where Seminary Road crosses 2nd
        Avenue and becomes Linden Lane, cross over and
        continue in the same direction (west) along the right
        side of Linden.

4.9-   At the next intersection, where Linden Lane
        diagonally crosses Brookville Road, continue
        straight on Linden.

4.5   Continue straight on Linden Lane across a bridge
        over the double-track CSX rail line and enter the
        Forest Glen Section of the Walter Reed Army
        Medical Center. (See Map 12-6.) (CAUTION:
        Linden Lane is narrow and busy, and there is no
        sidewalk after you cross the bridge over the
        railroad.)

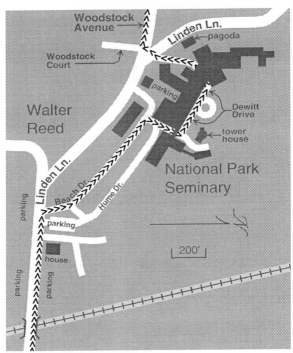

Map 12-6

The CSX line (originally a B&O line) connects Washington with Pittsburgh. The Walter Reed Army Medical Center is the U.S. Army's central medical facility. The main hospital grounds are located in northwest D.C. The Forest Glen Section houses mostly administrative and research facilities.

4.4   After crossing over the rail line, you will pass, in immediate succession on your right, a small parking area, then a clapboard house, then a small road, and then another parking area. A few steps past this last parking area, before Linden Lane turns diagonally to the right, turn right onto a small road. This is Beach Drive. You are now entering the grounds of what was once the National Park Seminary. (See Map 12-6.)

4.4-   In a short distance, at the first intersection, where Beach Drive meets Hume Drive, follow Beach Drive to the left. (See Map 12-6.)

The National Park Seminary was a junior college for women established in 1894 by John and Vesta Cassedy. The eclectic, fanciful style of the school buildings was a result of both design and chance -- design, because the Cassedys wanted to expose their students to the different architectural styles of the day, and chance, because they had no overall building plan for the school. Some of the most unusual buildings -- including a pagoda, a windmill, a Swiss chalet, and a castle -- were sorority houses. Over the years the original buildings were expanded and altered by subsequent owners. In particular, the original dark shingles and clapboard, which were perfectly suited to the wooded surroundings, have been covered with heavy stucco. The present owner is the U.S. Army, which took over the site during World War II to expand its medical facilities. Today, the future of the site is uncertain. Although the Army finds the old buildings inefficient and difficult to maintain, they are protected as historic landmarks in the National Register of Historic Places.

4.3   At the next intersection, where you come to a large, sprawling, complex-shaped stucco-and-wood building to your right, turn right and walk between two wings of the building and then under an archway connecting the wings. (See Map 12-6.)

4.3-   Past the archway, turn left and follow Dewitt Drive along the side of the building to your left. (See Map 12-6.)

4.3-   In a short distance, continue on Dewitt Drive, past a small traffic circle on your right. (See Map 12-6.)

Over the steps leading up to the building on your left is a stained glass sign reading "Ye Forest Inn." This building was originally a hotel and predates the National Park Seminary. The hotel was built by the Forest Glen Improvement Company, which had acquired the surrounding land in 1887 with the aim of developing a new suburban community. The company's plan was based on the recently established commuter service on the nearby B&O railroad, and the hotel was built to attract potential land buyers. After it became clear that the improvement company's

> *land development scheme was a failure, the Cassedys bought the land, including the hotel, for their school.*

4.3-   A few steps past the traffic circle, follow Dewitt Drive to the left into a tunnel through the building. (See Map 12-6.)

4.2   A short distance after leaving the tunnel, Dewitt Drive comes to an end at its intersection with Linden Lane. Cross Linden Lane here and then immediately turn to the right onto Woodstock Avenue, passing Woodstock Court on your left. (See Map 12-6.) (CAUTION: The is no crosswalk on Linden. Also, the first block of Woodstock Avenue is narrow, busy and has no sidewalk; make sure to walk on the left side.)

4.1   At the next intersection, where three roads enter Woodstock Avenue to your right, continue slightly to the left on Woodstock past the sign that says "NO OUTLET."

3.9   Where Woodstock Avenue ends at a traffic barrier at the edge of a woods, continue the hike into the woods on a well-used but unmarked dirt trail that begins just to the right of the traffic barrier. The trail turns to the left behind the barrier and then, in a short distance, descends to the right along a ridge line. (See Map 12-7, which shows topographic contour lines for every 50 feet of elevation.) (CAUTION: The trail descends steeply and may be slippery, especially when it is wet. Also, when there are fallen leaves on the ground, the route of the trail may not be clear.)

3.8   At the bottom of the hill, where the trail intersects a blacktop path, turn right onto the blacktop path. (See Map 12-7.)

3.7   Continue along the blacktop path onto a bridge over Rock Creek. (See Map 12-7.)

3.7-   A short distance after crossing the bridge, turn left onto an intersecting path that follows the left side of Jones Mill Road (unmarked when I was last here). (See Map 12-7.)

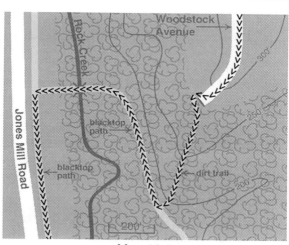

Map 12-7

If you look behind you here, you will see an unusual view of the spectacular towers of the Mormon Temple.

3.5   Continue on the path as it turns diagonally away from Jones Mill Road and enters a wooded area.

The parkland surrounding you is Rock Creek Regional Park. This park is an extension into Maryland of the better-known Rock Creek Park in the District of Columbia. Like Sligo Creek Park, Rock Creek Regional Park is another stream valley park established in the 1930s with federal assistance.

3.2   Where another blacktop path branches off to the right, bear to the left and, in a short distance, follow the path across a bridge over Rock Creek.

3.0   Pass under a high railroad trestle spanning the stream valley.

The railroad trestle is part of the abandoned B&O railroad branch line extending from Silver Spring in Maryland to the Georgetown waterfront in the District of Columbia. The branch line is presently being converted to a hiking and bicycle path known as the Capital Crescent Trail.

2.6   After passing through some open playing fields, the path comes to the traffic-light-controlled intersection

of East-West Highway and Meadowbrook Lane.
Cross East-West Highway at the crosswalk and, on
the other side, continue straight (south) down the
right side of Meadowbrook Lane. Soon, you will
pass a riding stable and paddocks on your right.

2.4   Immediately after passing the paddocks, follow
        Meadowbrook Lane (unmarked when I was last
        here) as it turns to the right (west) and becomes a
        smaller road. After you make this turn, the paddocks
        should still be on your right. (See Map 12-8.)

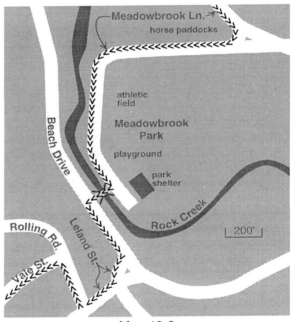

Map 12-8

2.1   A short distance after Meadowbrook Lane turns to
        the left (south), where there are a playground and a
        stone park shelter building on your left, turn right
        and cross Rock Creek on a footbridge. (See Map
        12-8.) The shelter building has public rest rooms
        and drinking water.

2.1-   After crossing the bridge over Rock Creek, continue
        straight across the intersecting road, Beach Drive,
        and, on the other side, climb a few steps and turn left
        onto the blacktop sidewalk. (See Map 12-8.)

2.0   A short distance down Beach Drive, at the first intersection, turn right onto Leland Street. (See Map 12-8.)

2.0-   In a short distance, where Leland Street intersects Rolling Road on your right, turn right onto Rolling Road. (See Map 12-8.)

1.9   In a short distance, where Rolling Road intersects Vale Street on your left, turn left onto Vale. (See Map 12-8.)

1.8   At the next intersection, where Vale Street meets Leland Street, turn right, back onto Leland.

1.5   After ascending and then descending a hill, at the intersection of Leland and Woodbine Streets, turn left onto Woodbine.

1.3   Cross Brookville Road and continue in the same direction on Woodbine.

1.1   Cross Connecticut Avenue and continue in the same direction on Woodbine. (CAUTION: Connecticut Avenue is a busy street with fast-moving traffic; cross at the traffic-light-controlled crosswalk a short distance to the left of Woodbine.)

On crossing Connecticut Avenue you enter the Town of Chevy Chase, Maryland. Founded in 1918 and developed primarily in the 1920s and 30s, the town was formed out of a corner of an earlier massive real estate empire controlled by the Chevy Chase Land Development Company. In the 1890s the development company amassed more than 1,700 acres of countryside along what would later be Connecticut Avenue, from Calvert Street in D.C. almost to what is now the Capital Beltway in Maryland. Then, to make the land accessible, the company, at its own expense, extended Connecticut Avenue through its property and built an electric streetcar line in the right-of-way. As in Takoma Park, an amusement park with a lake and a resort hotel was built to attract potential land buyers and to provide off-peak revenue for the streetcar line. The amusement park, known as Chevy Chase Lake, lay about half a mile farther north on Connecticut Avenue.

The hotel was a few blocks to the south. The amusement park and lake no longer exist and the hotel has become part of a national 4-H center. The principal founders of the development company were William Morris Stewart and Francis G. Newlands. Both, at different times, served as Senator from Nevada and both had substantial fortunes derived from silver and gold mining in the West.

1.0   At the next intersection, where Woodbine Street meets Meadow Lane, turn right onto Meadow Lane, and then, in a few steps, turn left, back onto Woodbine.

0.8   At the next intersection, where Woodbine Street meets Oak Lane, turn right onto Oak Lane. (See Map 12-9.)

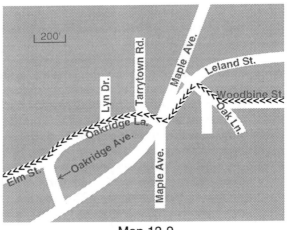

Map 12-9

0.8-   In a short distance, at the intersection of Oak Lane and Leland Street, turn left onto Leland. (See Map 12-9.)

0.7   In a short distance, where Leland Street intersects Maple Avenue to the left and Oakridge Lane to the right, turn right onto Oakridge Lane. (See Map 12-9.)

0.7-   In a few steps, where Tarrytown Road branches to the right, continue on Oakridge Lane to the left. (See Map 12-9.)

0.5   At the first stop sign, where Oakridge Avenue turns
        to the left and Elm Street turns slightly to the right,
        follow Elm Street to the right. (See Map 12-9.)

0.3   At the intersection of Elm Street and 46th Street to
        your left, continue straight on Elm, past the traffic
        barriers and through a park.

0.2   At the intersection of Elm Street and Wisconsin
        Avenue, cross and then turn right (north) onto
        Wisconsin Avenue.

        The area along Wisconsin Avenue here and down
        the connecting side streets offers one of the best
        selections of restaurants in the entire Washington
        area. The Bethesda Metro station and the end of the
        hike are just a short distance away, so, if you're
        interested, now is the time to start looking for a place
        to eat. A convenient and inexpensive place is the
        multi-shop Food Court just next to the Metro station
        itself. There are public rest rooms in the Food Court.

0.0   At the intersection of Wisconsin Avenue and Old
        Georgetown Road, you reach the principal entrance
        to the Bethesda Metro station and the end of the
        hike.

        *Bethesda usually refers to the commercial district
        and adjacent residential areas surrounding the
        intersection of Wisconsin Avenue and Old Georgetown
        Road. The name, taken from the Hebrew words for
        "house of mercy," was the name of an early 19th-
        century church located a little to the north along
        Wisconsin Avenue. Until recently, the commercial
        strip along Wisconsin Avenue consisted almost entirely
        of small low-rise shops. Today's intense, high-rise
        development has occurred almost entirely since (and
        presumably as a result of) the opening of the Metro
        station.*

NOTES